ABOUT THE EDITORS

LUCINDA EBERSOLE was born in Montana and grew up in Alabama. She is a writer, editor, and filmmaker. She recently completed a collection of short stories, tentatively titled *Death in Equality*.

RICHARD PEABODY is a native of Washington, D.C. He was editor/publisher of *Gargoyle* magazine for fourteen years. He is the author of three books of poetry, *I'm in Love with the Morton Salt Girl*, *Echt & Ersatz*, and *Sad Fashions*, and the editor of D.C. *Magazines: A Literary Retrospective* and *Mavericks: Nine Independent Publishers*.

MONDO Barbie

Edited by

Lucinda Ebersole & Richard Peabody

St.
Martin's
Press
New
York

MONDO BARBIE. Copyright © 1993 by Lucinda Ebersole and Richard
Peabody. All rights reserved. Printed in the United States of America.
No part of this book may be used or reproduced in any manner
whatsoever without written permission except in the case of brief
quotations embodied in critical articles or reviews. For information,
address St. Martin's Press, 175 Fifth Avenue, New York, N.Y. 10010.

Design by Jaye Zimet

Library of Congress Cataloging-in-Publication Data
Mondo Barbie / edited by Lucinda Ebersole and Richard Peabody
      p.   cm.
    ISBN 0-312-08848-5 (pbk.)
      1. Barbie dolls—Literary collections.   2. American Literature—
20th century.   I. Ebersole, Lucinda.   II. Peabody, Richard.
    PS509.B36M65   1993
  813'.018351—dc20   92-40820
                                                         CIP

First Edition: April 1993

10 9 8 7 6 5 4 3 2

CONTENTS

ACKNOWLEDGMENTS

Special thanks to: Barbara Benham, Mark Burgess, Ann Bur-
rola, Deanna D'errico, Christine Everly, Steve Feigenbaum,
Doug Fratz, Alan Friedman, Al Gabor, Sohrab Habibion,
Karla Hammond, James Harper, Nigel Hinshelwood, Derrick
Hsu, Siobahn Kelleher, Ron Kolm, Eleanor Lang, David Leh-
man, Doug Lewis, Ricia Mainhardt, Laura McGuff, Patrick
McKinnon, Katherine Meyer, Constance Pierce, Maja Praus-
nitz, Henry Richardson, Hugo Rizzoli, Rudy Rucker, Mary
Lynn Skutley, Silvana Straw, Dabrina Taylor, Lydia Tomkiw,
Cheryl Townsend, Phyllis & Michael Ward, Chris West, and
James Wu.

Sometimes I wish I was a pretty girl . . .
—Robyn Hitchcock

I wanna be Twist Barbie
—Shonen Knife

INTRODUCTION

Barbie is in the air, all right!

Since we began this anthology, we've seen articles on Barbie in magazines as wide-ranging as *Parenting*, *People*, and the *Utne Reader*. She's even in the current Maidenform commercials. We're not the only ones. Friends, acquaintances, and contributors (real and imagined) have flooded our mailboxes with clippings about Barbie look-alike contests, cable TV shows, photography exhibits, sculptures, you name it.

Everyone had an anecdote. One poet was sewing Barbie clothes when we called—no doubt an omen of good things to come. We heard Barbie dreams and Barbie fantasies, saw Barbie plays and Barbie movies, and listened to a vast and unique array of sexual confessions. We suffered through more poems and stories about Dan Quayle/Ken than any person should have to endure.

Stories and poems were just the tip of the Barbie toes. We read librettos by the groups Motor Totemist Guild and Forever Einstein. Performance artists in New York, Los Angeles, Toronto, and our own District of Columbia have incorporated Barbie dolls into their acts, but unfortunately, the material was strangely wanting when reduced to text on a page. That's why they call it "performance" art—you have to be there. Barbie and Ken turned up in DC Comics in *The Sandman*, but sadly, there was nothing we could isolate and use. We read Steve Abbott's screenplay *Revenge of the Barbies*, but again, there was no way to incorporate it into these pages.

Wild-goose chases were an everyday occurrence. A friend heard from a teacher who heard from a student who heard from a brother that a chapter in a famous novel talked about Barbie. Or maybe it was Ken. And now the novel is out of print, unless you're in England. A Terry Southern doll story never mentioned Barbie; Rudy Rucker's "Ken-Doll" character was too tangential for this book; Barbie is mentioned but has no particular influence on works by David Leavitt and Molly Hite. We were after something specific. The hours spent calling Canada to track down a story in *Pop Tart* magazine never did bear fruit. The Canadians kept asking why? Why Barbie?

Because Barbie is the problem. She is an American icon. The product of an adult fantasy of a girl-child's toy. Or is Barbie the adult's toy and the child's fantasy? What happens when the adult fantasy collides with the child's fantasy? Sparks fly. You would have no "Angry Women" issue of *RE/SEARCH* without Barbie. This book is the answer to millions of prayers. At last revealed—all that misplaced Barbie angst, all that childhood conditioning, torture, and repression. A home for brave Barbie survivors who can finally step forward. "My name is . . . and I had a Barbie."

We owe A. M. Homes and Denise Duhamel a debt of gratitude. For it was their readings at American University (same room, a year apart) that were the catalyst for this book. Rebecca Brown wrote a gem of a story on an impossible deadline. Ditto Cathryn Hankla and Lynne Barrett. Others were not so fortunate. We bemoan the exclusion of those who had previous commitments, were on vacation, didn't listen to their answering machines, or simply didn't make the grade. We are particularly saddened not to have had more input from writers of color. Another side of the Barbie coin yet to be explored.

In the end the book divided into two definite strategies for dealing with the Barbie phenomenon—poems and stories from Barbie's point of view, or writings about Barbie's impact (as either doll or flesh and blood) on specific characters. These works are just a sampling of the vast array of material inspired by Barbie. Perhaps, as one writer suggested, we should start a Barbie hot line. A way to reach all those warped by Barbie. A place for them to share their stories. A 1-800-4Barbie line.

Or perhaps a 1-900-4Barbie line. Talk live to your favorite Barbie, hear Barbie confess her most intimate secrets. That's what this book is all about. After all, everyone loves Barbie, don't they?

Lucinda Ebersole
Richard Peabody
March 1992

BARBIE DOLL

Marge Piercy

This girlchild was born as usual
and presented dolls that did pee-pee
and miniature GE stoves and irons
and wee lipsticks the color of cherry candy.
Then in the magic of puberty, a classmate said:
You have a great big nose and fat legs.

She was healthy, tested intelligent,
possessed strong arms and back,
abundant sexual drive and manual dexterity.
She went to and fro apologizing.
Everyone saw a fat nose on thick legs.

She was advised to play coy,
exhorted to come on hearty,
exercise, diet, smile and wheedle.
Her good nature wore out
like a fan belt.
So she cut off her nose and her legs
and offered them up.

In the casket displayed on satin she lay
with the undertaker's cosmetics painted on,
a turned-up putty nose,
dressed in a pink and white nightie.
Doesn't she look pretty? everyone said.
Consummation at last.
To every woman a happy ending.

A REAL DOLL

A. M. H o m e s

I'm dating Barbie. Three afternoons a week, while my sister is at dance class, I take Barbie away from Ken. I'm practicing for the future.

At first I sat in my sister's room watching Barbie, who lived with Ken, on a doily, on top of the dresser.

I was looking at her but not really looking. I was looking, and all of a sudden realized she was staring at me.

She was sitting next to Ken, his khaki-covered thigh absently rubbing her bare leg. He was rubbing her, but she was staring at me.

"Hi," she said.

"Hello," I said.

"I'm Barbie," she said, and Ken stopped rubbing her leg.

"I know."

"You're Jenny's brother."

I nodded. My head was bobbing up and down like a puppet on a weight.

"I really like your sister. She's sweet," Barbie said. "Such a good little girl. Especially lately, she makes herself so pretty, and she's started doing her nails."

I wondered if Barbie noticed that Miss Wonderful bit her nails and that when she smiled her front teeth were covered with little flecks of purple nail polish. I wondered if she knew Jennifer colored in the chipped chewed spots with purple Magic Marker, and then sometimes sucked on her fingers so that not only did she have purple flecks of polish on her teeth, but her tongue was the strangest shade of violet.

2

"So listen," I said. "Would you like to go out for a while? Grab some fresh air, maybe take a spin around the backyard?"

"Sure," she said.

I picked her up by her feet. It sounds unusual but I was too petrified to take her by the waist. I grabbed her by the ankles and carried her off like a Popsicle stick.

As soon as we were out back, sitting on the porch of what I used to call my fort, but which my sister and parents referred to as the playhouse, I started freaking. I was suddenly and incredibly aware that I was out with Barbie. I didn't know what to say.

"So, what kind of a Barbie are you?" I asked.

"Excuse me?"

"Well, from listening to Jennifer I know there's Day to Night Barbie, Magic Moves Barbie, Gift-Giving Barbie, Tropical Barbie, My First Barbie, and more."

"I'm Tropical," she said. I'm Tropical, she said, the same way a person might say I'm Catholic or I'm Jewish. "I came with a one-piece bathing suit, a brush, and a ruffle you can wear so many ways," Barbie squeaked.

She actually squeaked. It turned out that squeaking was Barbie's birth defect. I pretended I didn't hear it.

We were quiet for a minute. A leaf larger than Barbie fell from the maple tree above us and I caught it just before it would have hit her. I half expected her to squeak, "You saved my life. I'm yours, forever." Instead she said, in a perfectly normal voice, "Wow, big leaf."

I looked at her. Barbie's eyes were sparkling blue like the ocean on a good day. I looked and in a moment noticed she had the whole world, the cosmos, drawn in makeup above and below her eyes. An entire galaxy, clouds, stars, a sun, the sea, painted onto her face. Yellow, blue, pink, and a million silver sparkles.

We sat looking at each other, looking and talking and then not talking and looking again. It was a stop-and-start thing with both of us constantly saying the wrong thing, saying anything, and then immediately regretting having said it.

It was obvious Barbie didn't trust me. I asked her if she wanted something to drink.

"Diet Coke," she said. And I wondered why I'd asked.

3

I went into the house, upstairs into my parents' bathroom, opened the medicine cabinet, and got a couple of Valiums. I immediately swallowed one. I figured if I could be calm and collected, she'd realize I wasn't going to hurt her. I broke another Valium into a million small pieces, dropped some slivers into Barbie's Diet Coke, and swished it around so it'd blend. I figured if we could be calm and collected together, she'd be able to trust me even sooner. I was falling in love in a way that had nothing to do with love.

"So, what's the deal with you and Ken?" I asked later after we'd loosened up, after she'd drunk two Diet Cokes, and I'd made another trip to the medicine cabinet.

She giggled. "Oh, we're just really good friends."

"What's the deal with him really, you can tell me, I mean, is he or isn't he?"

"Ish she or ishn' she," Barbie said, in a slow slurred way, like she was so intoxicated that if they made a Breathalizer for Valium, she'd melt it.

I regretted having fixed her a third Coke. I mean if she OD'd and died, Jennifer would tell my mom and dad for sure.

"Is he a faggot or what?"

Barbie laughed and I almost slapped her. She looked me straight in the eye.

"He lusts after me," she said. "I come home at night and he's standing there, waiting. He doesn't wear underwear, you know. I mean, isn't that strange, Ken doesn't own any underwear. I heard Jennifer tell her friend that they don't even make any for him. Anyway, he's always there waiting, and I'm like, Ken, we're friends, okay, that's it. I mean, have you ever noticed, he has molded plastic hair. His head and his hair are all one piece. I can't go out with a guy like that. Besides, I don't think he'd be up for it if you know what I mean. Ken is not what you'd call well endowed. . . . All he's got is a little plastic bump, more of a hump, really, and what the hell are you supposed to do with that?"

She was telling me things I didn't think I should hear and all the same, I was leaning into her, like if I moved closer, she'd tell me more. I was taking every word and holding it for a minute, holding groups of words in my head like I didn't understand English. She went on and on, but I wasn't listening.

The sun sank behind the playhouse, Barbie shivered, excused herself, and ran around back to throw up. I asked her if she felt okay. She said she was fine, just a little tired, that maybe she was coming down with the flu or something. I gave her a piece of a piece of gum to chew and took her inside.

On the way back to Jennifer's room I did something Barbie almost didn't forgive me for. I did something which not only shattered the moment, but nearly wrecked the possibility of our having a future together.

In the hallway between the stairs and Jennifer's room, I popped Barbie's head into my mouth, like lion and tamer, God and Godzilla.

I popped her whole head into my mouth, and Barbie's hair separated into single strands like Christmas tinsel and caught in my throat nearly choking me. I could taste layer on layer of makeup, Revlon, Max Factor, and Maybelline. I closed my mouth around Barbie and could feel her breath in mine. I could hear her screams in my throat. Her teeth, white, Pearl Drops, Pepsodent, and the whole Osmond family, bit my tongue and the inside of my cheek like I might accidentally bite myself. I closed my mouth around her neck and held her suspended, her feet uselessly kicking the air in front of my face.

Before pulling her out, I pressed my teeth lightly into her neck, leaving marks Barbie described as scars of her assault, but which I imagined as a New Age necklace of love.

"I have never, ever in my life been treated with such utter disregard," she said as soon as I let her out.

She was lying. I knew Jennifer sometimes did things with Barbie. I didn't mention that once I'd seen Barbie hanging from Jennifer's ceiling fan, spinning around in great wide circles, like some imitation Superman.

"I'm sorry if I scared you."

"Scared me!" she squeaked.

She went on squeaking, a cross between the squeal when you let the air out of a balloon and a smoke alarm with weak batteries. While she was squeaking, the phrase *a head in the mouth is worth two in the bush* started running through my head. I knew it had come from somewhere, started as something else, but I couldn't get it right. *A head in the mouth is worth two in the bush*, again and again, like the punch line to some dirty joke.

"Scared me. Scared me. Scared me!" Barbie squeaked louder and louder until finally she had my attention again. "Have you ever been held captive in the dark cavern of someone's body?"

I shook my head. It sounded wonderful.

"Typical," she said. "So incredibly, typically male."

For a moment I was proud.

"Why do you have to do things you know you shouldn't, and worse, you do them with a light in your eye, like you're getting some weird pleasure that only another boy would understand. You're all the same," she said. "You're all Jack Nicholson."

I refused to put her back in Jennifer's room until she forgave me, until she understood that I'd done what I did with only the truest of feeling, no harm intended.

I heard Jennifer's feet clomping up the stairs. I was running out of time.

"You know I'm really interested in you," I said to Barbie.

"Me too," she said, and for a minute I wasn't sure if she meant she was interested in herself or me.

"We should do this again," I said. She nodded.

I leaned down to kiss Barbie. I could have brought her up to my lips, but somehow it felt wrong. I leaned down to kiss her and the first thing I got was her nose in my mouth. I felt like a St. Bernard saying hello.

No matter how graceful I tried to be, I was forever licking her face. It wasn't a question of putting my tongue in her ear or down her throat, it was simply literally trying not to suffocate her. I kissed Barbie with my back to Ken and then turned around and put her on the doily right next to him. I was tempted to drop her down on Ken, to mash her into him, but I managed to restrain myself.

"That was fun," Barbie said. I heard Jennifer in the hall.

"Later," I said.

Jennifer came into the room and looked at me.

"What?" I said.

"It's my room," she said.

"There was a bee in it. I was killing it for you."

"A bee. I'm allergic to bees. Mom, Mom," she screamed. "There's a bee."

"Mom's not home. I killed it."

"But there might be another one."

"So call me and I'll kill it."

"But if it stings me, I might die." I shrugged and walked out. I could feel Barbie watching me leave.

I took a Valium about twenty minutes before I picked her up the next Friday. By the time I went into Jennifer's room, everything was getting easier.

"Hey," I said when I got up to the dresser.

She was there on the doily with Ken, they were back to back, resting against each other, legs stretched out in front of them.

Ken didn't look at me. I didn't care.

"You ready to go?" I asked. Barbie nodded. "I thought you might be thirsty." I handed her the Diet Coke I'd made for her.

I'd figured Barbie could take a little less than an eighth of a Valium without getting totally senile. Basically, I had to give her Valium crumbs since there was no way to cut one that small.

She took the Coke and drank it right in front of Ken. I kept waiting for him to give me one of those I-know-what-you're-up-to-and-I-don't-like-it looks, the kind my father gives me when he walks into my room without knocking and I automatically jump twenty feet in the air.

Ken acted like he didn't even know I was there. I hated him.

"I can't do a lot of walking this afternoon," Barbie said. I nodded. I figured no big deal since mostly I seemed to be carrying her around anyway.

"My feet are killing me," she said.

I was thinking about Ken.

"Don't you have other shoes?"

My family was very into shoes. No matter what seemed to be wrong, my father always suggested it could be cured by wearing a different pair of shoes. He believed that shoes, like tires, should be rotated.

"It's not the shoes," she said. "It's my toes."

"Did you drop something on them?" My Valium wasn't working. I was having trouble making small talk. I needed another one.

"Jennifer's been chewing on them."

"What?"

"She chews on my toes."

"You let her chew your footies?"

I couldn't make sense out of what she was saying. I was thinking about not being able to talk, needing another or maybe two more Valiums, yellow adult-strength Pez.

"Do you enjoy it?" I asked.

"She literally bites down on them, like I'm flank steak or something," Barbie said. "I wish she'd just bite them off and have it over with. This is taking forever. She's chewing and chewing, more like gnawing at me."

"I'll make her stop. I'll buy her some gum, some tobacco or something, a pencil to chew on."

"Please don't say anything. I wouldn't have told you except . . ." Barbie said.

"But she's hurting you."

"It's between Jennifer and me."

"Where's it going to stop?" I asked.

"At the arch, I hope. There's a bone there, and once she realizes she's bitten the soft part off, she'll stop."

"How will you walk?"

"I have very long feet."

I sat on the edge of my sister's bed, my head in my hands. My sister was biting Barbie's feet off and Barbie didn't seem to care. She didn't hold it against her and in a way I liked her for that. I liked the fact she understood how we all have little secret habits that seem normal enough to us, but which we know better than to mention out loud. I started imagining things I might be able to get away with.

"Get me out of here," Barbie said. I slipped Barbie's shoes off. Sure enough, someone had been gnawing at her. On her left foot the toes were dangling and on the right, half had been completely taken off. There were tooth marks up to her ankles. "Let's not dwell on this," Barbie said.

I picked Barbie up. Ken fell over backwards and Barbie made me straighten him up before we left. "Just because you know he only has a bump doesn't give you permission to treat him badly," Barbie whispered.

I fixed Ken and carried Barbie down the hall to my room. I held Barbie above me, tilted my head back, and lowered her feet into my mouth. I felt like a young sword swallower practicing for my debut. I lowered Barbie's feet and legs into my mouth and then began sucking on them. They smelled like Jennifer and dirt and plastic. I sucked on her stubs and she told me it felt nice.

"You're better than a hot soak," Barbie said. I left her resting on my pillow and went downstairs to get us each a drink.

We were lying on my bed, curled into and out of each other. Barbie was on a pillow next to me and I was on my side facing her. She was talking about men, and as she talked I tried to be everything she said. She was saying she didn't like men who were afraid of themselves. I tried to be brave, to look courageous and secure. I held my head a certain way and it seemed to work. She said she didn't like men who were afraid of femininity, and I got confused.

"Guys always have to prove how boy they really are," Barbie said.

I thought of Jennifer trying to be a girl, wearing dresses, doing her nails, putting makeup on, wearing a bra even though she wouldn't need one for about fifty years.

"You make fun of Ken because he lets himself be everything he is. He doesn't hide anything."

"He doesn't have anything to hide," I said. "He has tan molded plastic hair, and a bump for a dick."

"I never should have told you about the bump."

I lay back on the bed. Barbie rolled over, off the pillow, and rested on my chest. Her body stretched from my nipple to my belly button. Her hands pressed against me, tickling me.

"Barbie," I said.

"Umm Humm."

"How do you feel about me?"

She didn't say anything for a minute. "Don't worry about it," she said, and slipped her hand into my shirt through the space between the buttons.

Her fingers were like the ends of the toothpicks performing some subtle ancient torture, a dance of boy death across my chest. Barbie crawled all over me like an insect who'd run into one too many cans of Raid.

Underneath my clothes, under my skin, I was going crazy. First off, I'd been kidnapped by my underwear with no way to manually adjust without attracting unnecessary attention.

With Barbie caught in my shirt I slowly rolled over, like in some space shuttle docking maneuver. I rolled onto my stomach, trapping her under me. As slowly and unobtrusively as possible, I ground myself against the bed, at first hoping it would fix things and then again and again, caught by a pleasure/pain principle.

"Is this a water bed?" Barbie asked.

My hand was on her breasts, only it wasn't really my hand, but more like my index finger. I touched Barbie and she made a little gasp, a squeak in reverse. She squeaked backwards, then stopped, and I was stuck there with my hand on her, thinking about how I was forever crossing a line between the haves and the have-nots, between good guys and bad, between men and animals, and there was absolutely nothing I could do to stop myself.

Barbie was sitting on my crotch, her legs flipped back behind her in a position that wasn't human.

At a certain point I had to free myself. If my dick was blue, it was only because it had suffocated. I did the honors and Richard popped out like an escape from maximum security.

"I've never seen anything so big," Barbie said. It was the sentence I dreamed of, but given the people Barbie normally hung out with, namely the bump boy himself, it didn't come as a big surprise.

She stood at the base of my dick, her bare feet buried in my pubic hair. I was almost as tall as she was. Okay, not almost as tall, but clearly we could be related. She and Richard even had the same vaguely surprised look on their faces.

She was on me and I couldn't help wanting to get inside her. I turned Barbie over and was on top of her, not caring if I killed her. Her hands pressed so hard into my stomach that it felt like she was performing an appendectomy.

I was on top, trying to get between her legs, almost

breaking her in half. But there was nothing there, nothing to fuck except a small thin line that was supposed to be her ass crack.

I rubbed the thin line, the back of her legs, and the space between her legs. I turned Barbie's back to me so I could do it without having to look at her face.

Very quickly, I came. I came all over Barbie, all over her and a little bit in her hair. I came on Barbie and it was the most horrifying experience I ever had. It didn't stay on her. It doesn't stick to plastic. I was finished. I was holding a come-covered Barbie in my hand like I didn't know where she came from.

Barbie said, "Don't stop," or maybe I just think she said that because I read it somewhere. I don't know anymore. I couldn't listen to her. I couldn't even look at her. I wiped myself off with a sock, pulled my clothes on, and then took Barbie into the bathroom.

At dinner I noticed Jennifer chewing her cuticles between bites of tuna-noodle casserole. I asked her if she was teething. She coughed and then started choking to death on either a little piece of fingernail, a crushed potato chip from the casserole, or maybe even a little bit of Barbie footie that'd stuck in her teeth. My mother asked her if she was okay.

"I swallowed something sharp," she said between coughs that were clearly influenced by the acting class she'd taken over the summer.

"Do you have a problem?" I asked her.

"Leave your sister alone," my mother said.

"If there are any questions to ask, we'll do the asking," my father said.

"Is everything all right?" my mother asked Jennifer. She nodded. "I think you could use some new jeans," my mother said. "You don't seem to have many play clothes anymore."

"Not to change the subject," I said, trying to think of a way to stop Jennifer from eating Barbie alive.

"I don't wear pants," Jennifer said. "Boys wear pants."

"Your grandma wears pants," my father said.

"She's not a girl."

My father chuckled. He actually fucking chuckled. He's the only person I ever met who could actually fucking chuckle.

"Don't tell her that," he said, chuckling.

"It's not funny," I said.

"Grandma's are pull-ons anyway," Jennifer said. "They don't have a fly. You have to have a penis to have a fly."

"Jennifer," my mother said. "That's enough of that."

I decided to buy Barbie a present. I was at that strange point where I would have done anything for her. I took two buses and walked more than a mile to get to Toys R Us.

Barbie row was aisle 14C. I was a wreck. I imagined a million Barbies and having to have them all. I pictured fucking one, discarding it, immediately grabbing a fresh one, doing it, and then throwing it into a growing pile in the corner of my room. An unending chore. I saw myself becoming a slave to Barbie. I wondered how many Tropical Barbies were made each year. I felt faint.

There were rows and rows of Kens, Barbies, and Skippers. Funtime Barbie, Jewel Secrets Ken, Barbie Rocker with "Hot Rockin' Fun and Real Dancin' Action." I noticed Magic Moves Barbie, and found myself looking at her carefully, flirtatiously, wondering if her legs were spreadable. "Push the switch and she moves," her box said. She winked at me while I was reading.

The only Tropical I saw was a black Tropical Ken. From just looking at him you wouldn't have known he was black. I mean, he wasn't black like anyone would be black. Black Tropical Ken was the color of a raisin, a raisin all spread out and unwrinkled. He had a short Afro that looked like a wig had been dropped down and fixed on his head, a protective helmet. I wondered if black Ken was really white Ken sprayed over with a thick coating of ironed raisin plastic.

I spread eight black Kens out in a line across the front of a row. Through the plastic window of his box he told me he was hoping to go to dental school. All eight black Kens talked at once. Luckily, they all said the same thing at the same time. They said he really liked teeth. Black Ken smiled.

He had the same white Pearl Drops, Pepsodent, Osmond family teeth that Barbie and white Ken had. I thought the entire Mattel family must take really good care of themselves. I figured they might be the only people left in America who actually brushed after every meal and then again before going to sleep.

I didn't know what to get Barbie. Black Ken said I should go for clothing, maybe a fur coat. I wanted something really special. I imagined a wonderful present that would draw us somehow closer.

There was a tropical pool and patio set, but I decided it might make her homesick. There was a complete winter holiday, with an A-frame house, fireplace, snowmobile, and sled. I imagined her inviting Ken away for a weekend without me. The six o'clock news set was nice, but because of her squeak, Barbie's future as an anchorwoman seemed limited. A workout center, a sofa bed and coffee table, a bubbling spa, a bedroom play set. I settled on the grand piano. It was $13.00. I'd always made it a point to never spend more than ten dollars on anyone. This time I figured, what the hell, you don't buy a grand piano every day.

"Wrap it up, would ya," I said at the checkout desk.

From my bedroom window I could see Jennifer in the backyard, wearing her tutu and leaping all over the place. It was dangerous as hell to sneak in and get Barbie, but I couldn't keep a grand piano in my closet without telling someone.

"You must really like me," Barbie said when she finally had the piano unwrapped.

I nodded. She was wearing a ski suit and skis. It was the end of August and eighty degrees out. Immediately, she sat down and played "Chopsticks."

I looked out at Jennifer. She was running down the length of the deck, jumping onto the railing and then leaping off, posing like one of those red flying horses you see on old Mobil gas signs. I watched her do it once and then the second time, her foot caught on the railing, and she went over the edge the hard way. A minute later she came around the edge of the house, limping, her tutu dented and dirty, pink tights ripped at both knees. I grabbed Barbie from the piano bench and raced her into Jennifer's room.

"I was just getting warmed up," she said. "I can play better than that, really."

I could hear Jennifer crying as she walked up the stairs.

"Jennifer's coming," I said. I put her down on the dresser and realized Ken was missing.

"Where's Ken?" I asked quickly.

"Out with Jennifer," Barbie said.

I met Jennifer at her door. "Are you okay?" I asked. She cried harder. "I saw you fall."

"Why didn't you stop me?" she said.

"From falling?"

She nodded and showed me her knees.

"Once you start to fall no one can stop you." I noticed Ken was tucked into the waistband of her tutu.

"They catch you," Jennifer said.

I started to tell her it was dangerous to go leaping around with a Ken stuck in your waistband, but you don't tell someone who's already crying that they did something bad.

I walked her into the bathroom, and took out the hydrogen peroxide. I was a first aid expert. I was the kind of guy who walked around, waiting for someone to have a heart attack just so I could practice my CPR technique.

"Sit down," I said.

Jennifer sat down on the toilet without putting the lid down. Ken was stabbing her all over the place and instead of pulling him out, she squirmed around trying to get comfortable like she didn't know what else to do. I took him out for her. She watched as though I was performing surgery or something.

"He's mine," she said.

"Take off your tights," I said.

"No," she said.

"They're ruined," I said. "Take them off."

Jennifer took off her ballet slippers and peeled off her tights. She was wearing my old Underoos with superheroes on them, Spiderman and Superman and Batman all poking out from under a dirty dented tutu. I decided not to say anything, but it looked funny as hell to see a flat crotch in boys' underwear. I had the feeling they didn't bother making underwear for Ken because they knew it looked too weird on him.

I poured peroxide onto her bloody knees. Jennifer screamed into my ear. She bent down and examined herself, poking her purple fingers into the torn skin; her tutu bunched up and rubbed against her face, scraping it. I worked on her knees, removing little pebbles and pieces of grass from the area.

She started crying again.

"You're okay," I said. "You're not dying." She didn't care. "Do you want anything?" I asked, trying to be nice.

"Barbie," she said.

It was the first time I'd handled Barbie in public. I picked her up like she was a complete stranger and handed her to Jennifer, who grabbed her by the hair. I started to tell her to ease up, but couldn't. Barbie looked at me and I shrugged. I went downstairs and made Jennifer one of my special Diet Cokes.

"Drink this," I said, handing it to her. She took four giant gulps and immediately I felt guilty about having used a whole Valium.

"Why don't you give a little to your Barbie," I said. "I'm sure she's thirsty too."

Barbie winked at me and I could have killed her, first off for doing it in front of Jennifer, and second because she didn't know what the hell she was winking about.

I went into my room and put the piano away. I figured as long as I kept it in the original box I'd be safe. If anyone found it, I'd say it was a present for Jennifer.

Wednesday Ken and Barbie had their heads switched. I went to get Barbie, and there on top of the dresser were Barbie and Ken, sort of. Barbie's head was on Ken's body and Ken's head was on Barbie. At first I thought it was just me.

"Hi," Barbie's head said.

I couldn't respond. She was on Ken's body and I was looking at Ken in a whole new way.

I picked up the Barbie head/Ken and immediately Barbie's head rolled off. It rolled across the dresser, across the white doily past Jennifer's collection of miniature ceramic cats, and *boom* it fell to the floor. I saw Barbie's head rolling and about to fall, and then falling, but there was nothing I could do to stop it. I was frozen, paralyzed with Ken's headless body in my left hand.

Barbie's head was on the floor, her hair spread out underneath it like angel wings in the snow, and I expected to see blood, a wide rich pool of blood, or at least a little bit coming out of her ear, her nose, or her mouth. I looked at her head on the floor and saw nothing but Barbie with eyes like the cosmos looking up at me. I thought she was dead.

"Christ, that hurt," she said. "And I already had a headache from these earrings."

There were little red dot/ball earrings jutting out of Barbie's ears.

"They go right through my head, you know. I guess it takes getting used to," Barbie said.

I noticed my mother's pin cushion on the dresser next to the other Barbie/Ken, the Barbie body, Ken head. The pin cushion was filled with hundreds of pins, pins with flat silver ends and pins with red, yellow, and blue dot/ball ends.

"You have pins in your head," I said to the Barbie head on the floor.

"Is that supposed to be a compliment?"

I was starting to hate her. I was being perfectly clear and she didn't understand me.

I looked at Ken. He was in my left hand, my fist wrapped around his waist. I looked at him and realized my thumb was on his bump. My thumb was pressed against Ken's crotch and as soon as I noticed I got an automatic hard-on, the kind you don't know you're getting, it's just there. I started rubbing Ken's bump and watching my thumb like it was a large-screen projection of a porno movie.

"What are you doing?" Barbie's head said. "Get me up. Help me." I was rubbing Ken's bump/hump with my finger inside his bathing suit. I was standing in the middle of my sister's room, with my pants pulled down.

"Aren't you going to help me?" Barbie kept asking. "Aren't you going to help me?"

In the second before I came, I held Ken's head hole in front of me. I held Ken upside down above my dick and came inside of Ken like I never could in Barbie.

I came into Ken's body and as soon as I was done I

wanted to do it again. I wanted to fill Ken and put his head back on, like a perfume bottle. I wanted Ken to be the vessel for my secret supply. I came in Ken and then I remembered he wasn't mine. He didn't belong to me. I took him into the bathroom and soaked him in warm water and Ivory liquid. I brushed his insides with Jennifer's toothbrush and left him alone in a cold-water rinse.

"Aren't you going to help me, aren't you?" Barbie kept asking.

I started thinking she'd been brain damaged by the accident. I picked her head up from the floor.

"What took you so long?" she asked.

"I had to take care of Ken."

"Is he okay?"

"He'll be fine. He's soaking in the bathroom." I held Barbie's head in my hand.

"What are you going to do?"

"What do you mean?" I said.

Did my little incident, my moment with Ken, mean that right then and there some decision about my future life as queerbait had to be made?

"This afternoon. Where are we going? What are we doing? I miss you when I don't see you," Barbie said.

"You see me every day," I said.

"I don't really see you. I sit on top of the dresser and if you pass by, I see you. Take me to your room."

"I have to bring Ken's body back."

I went into the bathroom, rinsed out Ken, blew him dry with my mother's blow dryer, then played with him again. It was a boy thing, we were boys together. I thought sometime I might play ball with him, I might take him out instead of Barbie.

"Everything takes you so long," Barbie said when I got back into the room.

I put Ken back up on the dresser, picked up Barbie's body, knocked Ken's head off, and smashed Barbie's head back down on her own damn neck.

"I don't want to fight with you," Barbie said as I carried her into my room. "We don't have enough time together to fight. Fuck me," she said.

I didn't feel like it. I was thinking about fucking Ken

and Ken being a boy. I was thinking about Barbie and Barbie being a girl. I was thinking about Jennifer, switching Barbie and Ken's heads, chewing Barbie's feet off, hanging Barbie from the ceiling fan, and who knows what else.

"Fuck me," Barbie said again.

I ripped Barbie's clothing off. Between Barbie's legs Jennifer had drawn pubic hair in reverse. She'd drawn it upside down so it looked like a fountain spewing up and out in great wide arcs. I spit directly onto Barbie and with my thumb and first finger rubbed the ink lines, erasing them. Barbie moaned.

"Why do you let her do this to you?"

"Jennifer owns me," Barbie moaned.

Jennifer owns me, she said, so easily and with pleasure. I was totally jealous. Jennifer owned Barbie and it made me crazy. Obviously it was one of those relationships that could only exist between women. Jennifer could own her because it didn't matter that Jennifer owned her. Jennifer didn't want Barbie, she had her.

"You're perfect," I said.

"I'm getting fat," Barbie said.

Barbie was crawling all over me, and I wondered if Jennifer knew she was a nymphomaniac. I wondered if Jennifer knew what a nymphomaniac was.

"You don't belong with little girls," I said.

Barbie ignored me.

There were scratches on Barbie's chest and stomach. She didn't say anything about them and so at first I pretended not to notice. As I was touching her, I could feel they were deep, like slices. The edges were rough; my finger caught on them and I couldn't help but wonder.

"Jennifer?" I said, massaging the cuts with my tongue, as though my tongue, like sandpaper, would erase them. Barbie nodded.

In fact, I thought of using sandpaper, but didn't know how I would explain it to Barbie: *you have to lie still and let me rub it really hard with this stuff that's like terry cloth dipped in cement.* I thought she might even like it if I made it into an S&M kind of thing and handcuffed her first.

I ran my tongue back and forth over the slivers, back and forth over the words "copyright 1966 Mattel Inc., Malaysia" tattooed on her back. Tonguing the tattoo drove Barbie crazy. She said it had something to do with scar tissue being extremely sensitive.

Barbie pushed herself hard against me, I could feel her slices rubbing my skin. I was thinking that Jennifer might kill Barbie. Without meaning to she might just go over the line and I wondered if Barbie would know what was happening or if she'd try to stop her.

We fucked, that's what I called it, fucking. In the beginning Barbie said she hated the word, which made me like it even more. She hated it because it was so strong and hard, and she said we weren't fucking, we were making love. I told her she had to be kidding.

"Fuck me," she said that afternoon and I knew the end was coming soon. "Fuck me," she said. I didn't like the sound of the word.

Friday when I went into Jennifer's room, there was something in the air. The place smelled like a science lab, a fire, a failed experiment.

Barbie was wearing a strapless yellow evening dress. Her hair was wrapped into a high bun, more like a wedding cake than something Betty Crocker would whip up. There seemed to be layers and layers of angel's hair spinning in a circle above her head. She had yellow pins through her ears and gold fuck-me shoes that matched the belt around her waist. For a second I thought of the belt and imagined tying her up, but more than restraining her arms or legs, I thought of wrapping the belt around her face, tying it across her mouth.

I looked at Barbie and saw something dark and thick like a scar rising up and over the edge of her dress. I grabbed her and pulled the front of the dress down.

"Hey, big boy," Barbie said. "Don't I even get a hello?"

Barbie's breasts had been sawed at with a knife. There were a hundred marks from a blade that might have had five rows of teeth like shark jaws. And as if that wasn't enough, she'd been dissolved by fire, blue and yellow flames had been pressed against her and held there until she melted and eventually became the fire that burned herself. All of it had been somehow stirred with the lead of a pencil, the point of a pen, and left to cool. Molten Barbie flesh had been left to harden, black and pink plastic swirled together, in the crater Jennifer had dug out of her breasts.

I examined her in detail like a scientist, a pathologist, a fucking medical examiner. I studied the burns, the gouged-out area, as if by looking closely I'd find something, an explanation, a way out.

A disgusting taste came up into my mouth, like I'd been sucking on batteries. It came up, then sank back down into my stomach, leaving my mouth puckered with the bitter metallic flavor of sour saliva. I coughed and spit onto my shirt sleeve, then rolled the sleeve over to cover the wet spot.

With my index finger I touched the edge of the burn as lightly as I could. The round rim of her scar broke off under my finger. I almost dropped her.

"It's just a reduction," Barbie said. "Jennifer and I are even now."

Barbie was smiling. She had the same expression on her face as when I first saw her and fell in love. She had the same expression she always had and I couldn't stand it. She was smiling, and she was burned. She was smiling, and she was ruined. I pulled her dress back up, above the scar line. I put her down carefully on the doily on top of the dresser and started to walk away.

"Hey," Barbie said, "aren't we going to play?"

MISS AMERICA 1990

Denise Duhamel

Miss Arizona roller-skates to "Amazing Grace,"
and Miss Pennsylvania thanks God for her kidney
    transplant.
How lucky and right for them to be here—smiling, as they
    remind us
about unfortunate discrimination against the hearing-
    impaired,
that it's so important for our youth to say no to drugs.
If we only recycled our bottles and cans, why
the world would be perfect, and they're here to prove it.
They're like cupcakes on a plate just for us,
like pheasants under the glass of our TV screens.
The "girls" have sliced off what they don't need—
extra fat on their noses, lumps jiggling
along their thighs. And they've pumped up
what they could use "just a tad" more of—
there's breast surgery and hairspray.
My friend Suzan-Lori says one of her first memories
in South Dakota was playing Playboy Bunny, strapping on ears
and hiking up her skirt. Who doesn't want to be
    desired? . . .
But she said she soon learned that no one could really love
    something
as flawless as Barbie. Her brother would unscrew
her dolls' heads, pull out their arms
by their tiny plastic sockets, and bury the parts
separately throughout the yard. And when my friend
        Pammy grew up

in Brooklyn, she didn't need a brother to give her
a realistic sense of what she could expect.
Her Kens used to jump off the roof
of the pink Dream House and attack the Barbies
who'd be casually strolling by. While in Ohio,
sheltered Carol had parents who said, "No daughter of
     mine
shall play with a Ken," so instead she and her sister
improvised with Skipper—They wound tape around
her junior-size breasts and cut off her hair
so she had to pose as a Casanova
with a short man's complex. And in Rhode Island,
kneeling under the Christmas tree,
I look up, smiling, but as though in a confused plea—
In this photo I have my fist around the feet
of my first shapely doll and, in the other hand,
a box of Russell Stover's chocolates. Believing, even then,
in all kinds of answers, I took a pin
to my Barbie's permanently lipsticked lips
and carefully, with an eyedropper, fed her milk.
I thought I couldn't identify until she looked more like me.
But with nowhere to expel my good intentions,
she began to smell sour, and my mother noticed—
I had to throw her out. So until my birthday
and more presents, I only had Midge. My grandmother
made her tiny raglan dresses. The low-cut gowns
in the store—almost as expensive as the dolls
     themselves . . .
My grandmother taught me, who needed them?
But we did have to compromise—
If my doll wanted to wear shoes at all,
she still had to wear those treacherous heels,
Midge's feet permanently arched to tiptoe. . . .
When my mother finally replaced my doll
it was with a dye-her-hair Barbie.
In one swoop of a sponge and a waft of ammonia,
she could be a bright blond, a redhead, or a brunette.
It was fun. I was happy.
And needless to say, Barbie, like Miss America, never went
     gray.

KINKY

Denise Duhamel

They decide to exchange heads.
Barbie squeezes the small opening under her chin
over Ken's bulging neck socket. His wide jaw line jostles
atop his girlfriend's body, loosely,
like one of those nodding novelty dogs
destined to gaze from the back windows of cars.
The two dolls chase each other around the orange Country
    Camper
unsure what they'll do when they're within touching
    distance.
Ken wants to feel Barbie's toes between his lips,
take off one of her legs and force his whole arm inside her.
With only the vaguest suggestion of genitals,
all the alluring qualities they possess as fashion dolls,
up until now have done neither of them much good.
But suddenly Barbie is excited looking at her own body
under the weight of Ken's face. He is part circus freak,
part thwarted hermaphrodite. And she is imagining
she is somebody else—maybe somebody middle-class and
    ordinary,
maybe another teenage model being caught in a scandal.

The night had begun with Barbie getting angry
at finding Ken's blow-up doll, folded and stuffed
under the couch. He was defensive and ashamed, especially
    about
not even having the breath to inflate her. But after a
    round

of pretend-tears, Barbie and Ken vowed to try
to make their relationship work. With their good memories
as sustaining as good food, they listened to late-night radio
talk shows, one featuring Doctor Ruth. *When all else fails,*
just hold each other, the small sex therapist crooned.
Barbie and Ken, on cue, groped in the dark,
their interchangeable skin glowing, the color of Band-Aids.
Then, they let themselves go—Soon Barbie was begging
     Ken
to try on her Spandex miniskirt. She showed him how
to pivot as though he was on a runway. Ken begged
to tie Barbie onto his yellow surfboard, blindfold and spin
her on the kitchen table until she grew dizzy. *Anything,*
anything, they both said to the other's requests,
their mirrored desires bubbling from the most unlikely
     places.

ASTROLOGY BARBIE

Denise Duhamel

Barbie is a Pisces,
born during the last sign of the zodiac.
Like others under the influence
of the wide seas, she's addicted to make-believe,
giving up childhood only when she absolutely has to.
When she was young, her astrologer told her that,
though she didn't desire money or fame,
Barbie'd have both someday. Advised that if
she worked hard,
Barbie's potential for combining the material world
with her inspired philosophical vision
would be tremendous. The doll surrounded herself
with her birthstones: aquamarine,
ivory, and jade, and waited for romance.
According to the stars, she'd be drawn
to those handicapped
in some way—a man in a wheelchair, maybe a partner
without a penis. When she met Ken (a younger doll,
by two years)—
born under the year of the Ox,
the second sign in the Chinese zodiac—she knew
he would be tender, but never romantic.
Because she was a compatible Pig, a symbol
with kinder connotations in the East, Barbie
quickly got in touch with the authoritative
side of her nature. She decided that she and Ken
would be good mates, reading their horoscopes every day,
their personality quirks rubbing against the cosmos.

Sometimes they were chafed. Sometimes it felt good.
Over pretend-tea, they often argued, good-naturedly,
about determinism versus free will. Sometimes
they were separated by children and tossed
into different toy chests. Other times, they lay
all night in one another's arms, true blue
as soul mates or Elvis Presley songs.

IT'S MY BODY

Denise Duhamel

"There was a time when Barbie couldn't even
bend her knees," I tell my nieces Kerri and Katie
who sit before me on a living room floor
in blue-and-pink-collar America.
They are strapping their Rock-n-Roll Barbies
into tiny Leatherette pants
and big black guitars
with jagged lightning hips. Katie hands me
her doll because she needs help
with the teeny buttons that snake the back
of Barbie's off-the-shoulder blouse. "My first Barbie
couldn't even twist her waist." I am talking
like a person who has lived long enough
to see significant change. My nieces
have their backs to the TV which seems always on,
wherever I am. And behind their blond
innocent heads, Jessica Hahn
makes a cameo appearance on an MTV video.
She rolls like a sexy pinball,
then tries to claw herself out of a concave cage.
"It's my body," I recently heard her say
on a morning talk show. She started
by defending her nude poses in *Playboy*.
"It's my body," she repeated
like a Chatty Cathy doll
with a skipping record stuck in her back.
"It's my body," she began to answer
her interviewer's every inquiry—

where she grew up, if she still went to church.
"It's my body?"
The words stayed the same,
but as more accusations came, her inflections
changed. Jessica looked beyond the studio set
where someone seemed to be cueing her
that message. My lover was laughing.
"How about a little conviction there, Jessica?"
he said to the TV. Then, trying to coax
more conversation, he addressed me: "Look,
honey, she doesn't even seem to know if it's her body
or not." He was right,
but he knew as he brought it up,
it was the wrong thing to say.
I'd had too much coffee.
I found myself energetically defending Jessica,
blaming her disorientation
as a response to our misogynous society—
the dislocation all women
feel from their physical selves.
And then came the theories I'd been reading.
He left for work kind of agreeing
but also complaining that I'd made him exhausted.
And now my sister is blaming me for the same thing
because I am pointing out to Katie that she is mistaken
to think only boys should get dirty
and only girls should wear earrings.
"People should be able to do whatever they want."
I lecture her about my friend who wears a hard hat
when she goes to her job and works
with electricity just like her daddy.
Katie fiddles with her shoelaces
and asks for juice. My sister says,
"Give the kid a break. She's only in kindergarten."
Older Kerri is concentrating, trying
to get a big comb for humans
through her doll's moussed synthetic hair.
Because untangling the snarls needs so much force,
suddenly, accidentally, Barbie's head pops off,
and a smaller one, a faceless socket,
emerges from her neck. For an instant

we all—two sets of sisters, our ages
twenty years apart—share a small epiphany
about Mattel: this brainwashed piece of plastic cerebrum
is underneath who Barbie is. But soon
Kerri's face is all panic, like she will be punished.
The tears begin in the corners of her eyes.
I make a fast rescue attempt,
spearing Barbie's molded head
back on her body, her malleable features distorting
under my thumb. Although a grown doll,
the soft spot at the top of her skull
still hasn't closed. Under the pressure
of my touch, her face is squashed, someone
posing in a fun house mirror.
But the instant I let go, she snaps back
into a polite smile, her small perfect nose
erect and ready to make everything
right: Barbie is America's—
half victim, half little pink soldier.

BARBIE-Q

FOR LICHA

Sandra Cisneros

ours is the one with mean eyes and a ponytail. Striped swimsuit, stilettos, sunglasses, and gold hoop earrings. Mine is the one with bubble hair. Red swimsuit, stilettos, pearl earrings, and a wire stand. But that's all we can afford, besides one extra outfit apiece. Yours, "Red Flair," sophisticated A-line coatdress with a Jackie Kennedy pillbox hat, white gloves, handbag, and heels included. Mine, "Solo in the Spotlight," evening elegance in black glitter strapless gown with a puffy skirt at the bottom like a mermaid tail, formal-length gloves, pink chiffon scarf, and mike included. From so much dressing and undressing, the black glitter wears off where her titties stick out. This and a dress invented from an old sock when we cut holes here and here and here, the cuff rolled over for the glamorous, fancy-free, off-the-shoulder look.

Every time the same story. Your Barbie is roommates with my Barbie, and my Barbie's boyfriend comes over and your Barbie steals him, okay? Kiss kiss kiss. Then the two Barbies fight. You dumbbell! He's mine. Oh no he's not, you stinky! Only Ken's invisible, right? Because we don't have money for a stupid-looking boy doll when we'd both rather ask for a new Barbie outfit next Christmas. We have to make do with your mean-eyed Barbie and my bubblehead Barbie and our one outfit apiece not including the sock dress.

Until next Sunday when we are walking through the flea market on Maxwell Street and *there!* Lying on the street next to some tool bits, and platform shoes with the heels all squashed, and a fluorescent green wicker wastebasket, and aluminum foil, and hubcaps, and a pink shag rug, and windshield wiper blades, and dusty mason jars, and a coffee can full of rusty nails. *There!* Where? Two Mattel boxes. One with the "Career Gal" ensemble, snappy black-and-white business suit, three-quarter-length sleeve jacket with kick-pleat skirt, red sleeveless shell, gloves, pumps, and matching hat included. The other, "Sweet Dreams," dreamy pink-and-white plaid nightgown and matching robe, lace-trimmed slippers, hairbrush and hand mirror included. How much? Please, please, please, please, please, please, please, until they say okay.

On the outside you and me skipping and humming but inside we are doing loopity-loops and pirouetting. Until at the next vendor's stand, next to boxed pies, and bright orange toilet brushes, and rubber gloves, and wrench sets, and bouquets of feather flowers, and glass towel racks, and steel wool, and Alvin and the Chipmunks records, *there!* And *there!* And *there!* And *there!* and *there!* and *there!* and *there!* Bendable Legs Barbie with her new pageboy hairdo. Midge, Barbie's best friend. Ken, Barbie's boyfriend. Skipper, Barbie's little sister. Tutti and Todd, Barbie and Skipper's tiny twin sister and brother. Skipper's friends, Scooter and Ricky. Alan, Ken's buddy. And Francie, Barbie's MOD'ern cousin.

Everybody today selling toys, all of them damaged with water and smelling of smoke. Because a big toy warehouse on Halsted Street burned down yesterday—see there?—the smoke still rising and drifting across the Dan Ryan expressway. And now there is a big fire sale at Maxwell Street, today only.

So what if we didn't get our new Bendable Legs Barbie and Midge and Ken and Skipper and Tutti and Todd and Scooter and Ricky and Alan and Francie in nice clean boxes and had to buy them on Maxwell Street, all water-soaked and sooty. So what if our Barbies smell like smoke when you hold them up to your nose even after you wash and wash and wash them. And if the prettiest doll, Barbie's MOD'ern cousin Francie with real eyelashes, eyelash brush included, has a left foot that's melted a little—so? If you dress her in her new "Prom Pinks" outfit, satin splendor with matching coat, gold belt, clutch, and hair bow included, so long as you don't lift her dress, right?—who's to know.

PLAYING WITH BARBIE

Jeanne Beaumont

*Playing with Barbie, a young girl
could discover the world of modeling,
adventure, and those mysteries such as
lingerie, jewelry, hairstyles, and makeup.*

A. Glenn Mandeville

The breasts, the breasts
like my first two knuckles when I made a fist
and then the teensy waspy waist,
narrow hips and legs as long as—
chopsticks—I never liked her face,
that is, it wasn't pretty:
her eyes too darkly lidded, shifty,
aimed down to the right and big-irised
as though her ponytail, pulled too tight,
had made them pop. Her nose, it must be
pointed out, was much too small
as were her feet—high-heeled, tiptoed,
so that she couldn't stand on her own
(for several years I supported her).

Her real attraction was wardrobe,
the minute perfections of her clothes
like adulthood stitched diminutive,
fur collars, satin linings, lace.
I choked her neck with pearls, topped her
with hats, gave her a lamé purse to clasp—

I never gave her Ken.
I made up my own pubescent breed of men
to escort her, and there was Midge
to keep her company at night when
I tucked her into the plastic place
and, model maid, boxed her accessories,
hung up her clothes, and packed her case.

Now when I open that girlhood shrine
sealed in the attic for so long,
she's clean, she's waiting,
she fits again right in my hand
—and I'm King Kong.

BARBIE

Gary Soto

The day after Christmas, Veronica Solis and her babysister, Yolanda, nestled together on the couch to watch the morning cartoons. Bumbling Inspector Gadget was in trouble again, unaware that the edge of the cliff was crumbling under his feet. Soon he was sliding down the mountain toward a pit of alligators. He commanded, "Go, go, gadget umbrella," and a red umbrella popped out of his hat. He landed safely just a few feet from a dark green alligator and dusted himself off.

Veronica liked this show, but she was really waiting for the next one: "My Little Pony." That show had lots of Barbie commercials and Veronica was in love with Barbie, her blond hair, her slim waist and long legs, and the glamorous clothes on tiny hangers. She had wanted a Barbie for as long as she could remember and almost got one last Christmas, but her Uncle Rudy, who had more money than all her other uncles combined, bought her the worst kind of doll, an imitation Barbie.

Veronica had torn the silver wrapping off her gift and found a black-haired doll with a flat, common nose, not like Barbie's cute, upturned nose. She had wanted to cry, but she gave her uncle a hug, forced a smile, and went to her bedroom to stare at the doll. A tear slid down her cheek.

"You ugly thing," she snapped, and threw the imposter against the wall. The doll lay on the floor, eyes open like the dead. Immediately, Veronica felt ashamed. She picked up the doll and set it beside her.

"I'm sorry. I don't hate you," she whispered. "It's just

that you're not a *real* Barbie." She noticed that the forehead was chipped where it had struck the wall, and that one of the eyelashes was peeling off like a scab.

"Oh, no," she gasped. Veronica tried to push the eyelash back into place, but it came off and stuck to her thumb. "Doggone it," she mumbled, and returned to the living room, where her uncle was singing Mexican Christmas songs.

He stopped to sip from his coffee cup and pat Veronica's hand. "Did you name your doll yet?"

"No, not yet." Veronica looked at the floor. She hoped that he wouldn't ask her to bring it out.

"Let's see her. I'll sing her a song," he teased.

Veronica didn't want him to see that the doll's face was chipped and one of her eyelashes was gone.

"She's asleep," she said.

"Well, in that case, we'll let her sleep," he said. "I'll sing her a lullaby, 'Rock-a-Bye-Baby' in Spanish."

That was last year. There had been no Barbie this Christmas either. Today was just a cold winter morning in front of the television.

Her Uncle Rudy came over to the house with his girlfriend, Donna. Veronica's mother was uneasy. Why was the girlfriend here? Was this the moment? She dried her hands on a kitchen towel and told the children to go play outside. She turned to the woman and, ignoring her brother, asked, "What'd you get for Christmas?"

"A robe and slippers," she said, looking at Rudy, then added, "and a sweatsuit from my brother."

"Come, have a seat. I'll start coffee."

"Helen, would you call Veronica back inside?" Rudy asked. "We have an extra present for her."

"Okay," she said, hurrying to the kitchen, her face worried because something was up and it could be marriage. She called, "Veronica, your uncle wants you."

Veronica dropped her end of the jump rope, leaving her sister and brother to carry on without her. She walked back into the house and stood by her uncle; but she couldn't take her eyes off the woman.

"How's school?" asked her uncle.

"Fine," she said shyly.

"Getting good grades?"

"Pretty good."

"As good as the boys? Better?"

"Lots better."

"Any *novios?*"

Donna slapped Rudy's arm playfully. "Rudy, quit teasing the child. Give it to her."

"Okay," he said, patting Donna's hand. He turned to Veronica. "I have something for you. Something I know you wanted."

Uncle Rudy's girlfriend reached in a package at her feet and brought out a Barbie doll in a striped, one-piece swimsuit. "This is for you, honey."

Veronica stared at the woman, then at the doll. The woman's eyes were almost as blue, and her hair almost as blond as Barbie's. Veronica slowly took the Barbie from the woman and very softly said, "Thank you." She gave her uncle a big hug, taking care not to smash Barbie against his chest. Veronica smiled at the woman, then at her mother, who returned from the kitchen with a pot of coffee and a plate of powdery-white donuts.

"Look, Mom, a Barbie," Veronica said happily.

"Oh, Rudy, you're spoiling this girl," Mrs. Solis chided.

"And that's not all," Rudy said. "Donna, show her the clothes."

The woman brought out three outfits: a summer dress, a pants suit, and a lacy gown the color of mother-of-pearl.

"They're lovely!" said the mother. She held the summer dress up and laughed at how tiny it was.

"I like them a lot," said Veronica. "It's just like on TV."

The grown-ups sipped their coffee and watched Veronica inspect the clothes. After a few minutes Rudy sat up and cleared his throat.

"I have something to say," he said to his sister, who already suspected what it was. "We're getting married—soon."

He patted Donna's hand, which sported a sparkling ring, and announced a second time that he and Donna were getting married. The date wasn't set yet, but they would have their wedding in the spring. Veronica's mother, feigning surprise, lifted her eyes and said, "Oh, how wonderful! Oh, Rudy—and Donna." She kissed her brother and the woman.

"Did you hear, Veronica? Your uncle is going to get married." She hesitated, then added, "To Donna."

Veronica pretended to look happy, but she was too preoccupied with her new doll.

In her bedroom Veronica hugged her Barbie and told her she was beautiful. She combed Barbie's hair with a tiny blue comb and dressed her in the three outfits. She made believe that Barbie was on a lunch date with a girlfriend from work, the fake Barbie with the chipped forehead and missing eyelash.

"Oh, look—boys!" the ugly doll said. "They're so cute."

"Oh, those boys," Barbie said coolly. "They're okay, but Ken is so much more handsome. And richer."

"They're good-looking to me. I'm not as pretty as you, Barbie."

"That's true," Barbie said. "But I still like you. How's your sandwich?"

"Good, but not as good as your sandwich," the ugly doll answered.

Veronica was eager to make Barbie the happiest person in the world. She dressed her in her swimsuit and said in a fake English accent, "You look smashing, my child."

"And who are you going to marry?" the fake Barbie asked.

"The king," she announced. Veronica raised Barbie's movable arms. "The king is going to buy me a yacht and build me a swimming pool." Veronica made Barbie dive into an imaginary pool. "The king loves me more than money. He would die for me."

Veronica played in her room all afternoon, and the next day called her friend Martha. Martha had two Barbies and one Ken. She invited Veronica to come over to play Barbies, and play they did. The three Barbies went to Disneyland and Magic Mountain and ate at an expensive restaurant where they talked about boys. Then all three took turns kissing Ken.

"Ken, you kiss too hard," Martha giggled.

"You forgot to shave," whined Veronica.

"Sorry," Ken said.

"That's better," they said, laughing, and clacked the dolls' faces together.

But at the end of the day the two girls got into an argument when Martha tried to switch the Barbies so she would get Veronica's newer Barbie. Veronica saw that Martha was trying to trick her and pushed her against the bureau, yelling, "You stupid cheater!" She left with her three outfits and Barbie under her arm.

At the corner she hugged and kissed Barbie. "That's the last time we're going to her house," said Veronica. "She almost stole you."

She sat on the curb, dressed Barbie in her pants suit, then walked through an alley where she knew there was an orange tree. She stopped under the tree, which was heavy with oranges the size of softballs, and swiped one.

As she walked home she peeled the orange with her polish-chipped nails and looked around the neighborhood. With her Barbie doll pressed under her arm, she was happy. The day was almost over, and soon she and Barbie would be sitting down to dinner. After she finished the orange, she wiped her hands on her pants and started to play with Barbie.

"Oh, it's a beautiful day to look pretty," Barbie said. "Yes, I'm going to—"

Veronica stopped in midsentence. Barbie's head was gone. Veronica waved her hand over the space where a smile and blond hair had been only a few minutes ago.

"Darn it," she hissed. "Her head's gone."

She fell to one knee and felt around. She picked up ragged leaves, loose dirt, and bottle caps. "Where is it?" She checked the leaf-choked gutter and raked her hand through the weeds along a fence. She slowly retraced her steps into the alley, desperately scanning the ground. She looked at the headless Barbie in her hand. She wanted to cry but knew it would just make her eyes blurry.

"Where are you?" Veronica called to the head. "Please let me find you."

She came to the orange tree. She got down and searched on all fours, but found nothing. She pounded the ground with her fists and burst into tears.

"She's ruined," Veronica sobbed. "Oh, Barbie, look at you. You're no good anymore." She looked through her tears at Barbie and got mad. How could Barbie do this to her after only one day?

For the next hour she searched the street and the alley. She even knocked on Martha's door and asked her if she had seen Barbie's head.

"No," Martha said. She kept the door half-closed because she was afraid that Veronica was still mad at her for trying to switch their Barbies. "Did you lose it?"

"It just fell off. I don't know what happened. It was brand-new."

"How did it fall off?"

"How do I know? It just fell off. Stupid thing!"

Veronica looked so distressed that Martha went outside and helped her look, assuring Veronica that together they would find the head.

"One time I lost my bike keys at the playground," Martha said. "I just looked and looked. I just got on my knees and crawled around. Nobody helped me. I found them all by myself."

Veronica ignored Martha's chatter. She was busy parting weeds with her hands and overturning rocks and boards under which the head might have rolled. After a while Veronica had a hard time concentrating and had to keep reminding herself what she was looking for. "Head," she said, "look for the head." But everything became jumbled together. She stared at the ground so long that she couldn't tell an eggshell from a splintered squirt gun.

If only it could talk, wished Veronica, who was once again on the verge of tears. If only it could yell, "Over here, I'm here by the fence. Come and get me." She blamed herself, then Martha. If they hadn't had that argument, everything would have been all right. She would have played and then returned home. She probably jinxed her Barbie when she pushed Martha against the chest of drawers. Maybe that was when Barbie's head had come loose; she had been holding Barbie while she fought Martha.

When it began to get dark Martha said she had to go. "But I'll help you tomorrow if you want," she said.

Veronica puckered her mouth and shouted, "It's all your fault! You made me mad. You tried to cheat me. My Barbie was more beautiful than yours, and now see what you've done!" She held the headless Barbie up for Martha to see. Martha turned away and ran.

That night Veronica sat in her room. She felt that she had betrayed Barbie by not caring for her and couldn't stand to look at her. She wanted to tell her mother, but she knew Mom would scold her for being a *mensa*.

"If only I could tell Uncle Rudy's girlfriend," she said. "She would understand. She would do something."

Finally, Veronica dressed in her nightie, brushed her teeth, and jumped into bed. She started reading a library book about a girl in New York City who had lost her cat, but tossed it aside because the words on the page meant nothing. It was a made-up story, while her own sadness was real.

"I shouldn't have gone," said Veronica, staring at the ceiling. "I should have stayed home and played by myself."

She sat up and tried to read again, but she couldn't concentrate. She picked at a scab on her wrist and tried to lull herself to sleep with sad thoughts. When she couldn't stand it anymore, she kicked off the blankets and walked over to her Barbie, which lay on a chest of drawers. She picked up the fake Barbie, too.

"Let's go to sleep," she whispered to both dolls, and carried them lovingly to bed.

BARBIE'S FERRARI

L y n n e   M c M a h o n

Nothing is quite alien or quite recognizable at this speed,
Though there is the suggestion of curve, a mutant
Curvature designed, I suppose, to soften or offset
The stiletto toes and karate arms that were too
Angular for her last car, a Corvette as knifed as Barbie
Herself, and not the bloodred of Italian Renaissance.
This is Attention. This is detail fitted to sheer
Velocity. For her knees, after all, are locked—
Once fitted into the driving pit, she can only accelerate
Into a future that becomes hauntingly like the past:
Nancy Drew in her yellow roadster, a convertible,
I always imagined, the means to an end
Almost criminal in its freedom, its motherlessness.
For Barbie, too, is innocent of parents, pressing
Her unloved breasts to the masculine wheel, gunning
The turn into the hallway and out over the maiming stairs,
Every jolt slamming her uterus into uselessness, sealed,
Sealed up and preserved, everything about her becoming
Pure Abstraction and the vehicle for Desire: to be Nancy,
To be Barbie, to feel the heaven of Imagination
Breathe its ether on your cheeks, rosying in the slipstream
As the speedster/roadster/Ferrari plummets over the rail
Into the ocean of waxed hardwood below.
To crash and burn
And be retrieved. To unriddle the crime. To be
Barbie with a plot! That's the soulful beauty of it.
That's the dreaming child.
Not the dawn of Capital, the factories of Hong Kong

Reversing the currency in Beijing. Not the ovarian
Moon in eclipse. Just the dreaming child, the orphan,
Turning in slow motion in the air above the bannister,
For whom ideas of gender and marketplace are nothings
Less than nothing. It's the car she was born for.
It's Barbie you mourn for.

THICKER THAN WATER

Kathryn Harrison

One summer, my grandparents enrolled me in an urban day camp. Fifty or so children, all culled from Los Angeles prep schools, were gathered into vans on Mondays, Wednesdays, and Fridays, at nine in the morning, and taken to edifying places. The tar pits, the art museum. Children's theater in MacArthur Park, the Griffith Park Observatory. I didn't want to go to camp, but this was a compromise of sorts between a sleep-away and nothing at all, so I went. I liked the tar pits, the sorrowing old bones of the dinosaurs buried in the flat oily lake, the acrid smell of the tar in the summer heat of the city. There was a fence around the pits, to keep children from that same wallowing, slow death, I imagined, and the grass grew yellow and sickly at the black edge of the ancient lake.

We visited a few industrial amusement parks as well: Wonder bread, and Busch Gardens, where we took a monorail through the brewery and watched bottles being filled, my head swimming with the thick smell of the hops.

One Friday, we drove miles to get to the Mattel toy factory, which was far away from the Los Angeles I knew. Deep in the industrial south of the city, it had a huge red sign turning slowly over the freeway that said, for the girls, HOME OF BARBIE on one side and, for the boys, HOME OF HOT WHEELS on the other.

In my own bedroom I had an immense distance, about fifteen yards, of orange track laid down, and ten little cars that I sped over it and wrecked dramatically—especially on the steep descent from the top of the bureau. I was hoping we would get a free tiny Corvette or dune buggy when we finished the tour. After all, Wonder bread had given us each a miniature loaf of doughy white bread which I found too cunning to unwrap and eat; it was now on the patio, green with mold.

I liked the inside of factories, I loved conveyor belts and the shining competent machines, the workers all in the same uniforms. I wanted to see how Mattel made the little cars. But when we got inside, the boys were separated into their own group and led away, the girls forced to follow a large blond woman to the doll injection molds.

I never liked dolls, but even if I had, that afternoon's entertainment would have put me off them forever. A huge vent blew hundreds of disembodied, bald heads, fashioned from fleshy plastic, onto a conveyor belt from which droves of big black women snatched each one up and ran it under the needle of a monstrous sewing machine and stitched a mop of colored plastic hair onto its head. They threw them, about a hundred a minute, back onto the rolling endless belt from which other workers grabbed them and quickly painted eyes and a pink smile onto their little molded features. Thus enlivened, all the heads tumbled along the belt and joined the flow of necks and torsos, the two tributaries forming a giant pink river of body parts.

I stared, horror-struck, as heads were jammed onto necks, given a twist by a large hand so that they faced forward, and then pitched into a great rolling hamper that took the little quadriplegic figures on to the arms-and-legs section, where limbs were forced into appropriate holes.

The workers, most of them huge women weighing at least two hundred pounds, their hair tied back in regulation pink nets, their bulk swathed in immense pink aprons, never looked up from the carnage that flowed before them. Their hands were a blur of productivity, articulating tiny joints. Every once in a while a doll would come out wrong, legless, perhaps, or otherwise handicapped, and she would be dismembered, her parts thrown by the doll-undoer into various separate bins.

Once assembled, the river of naked Barbies flowed on to be clothed, their huge breasts and minuscule arched feet and wasp waists all jumbling together. First, a pair of tiny, flimsy underpants, and a frothy blue party dress and matching plastic pumps. Hair was combed back into demure flips, secured with clear polyurethane bands, and then each doll was ready to be laid in a little paper and plastic casket with her name on it, and sealed into a package for the stores.

I fainted with fear at the end of the excursion. Or at least, I sat down suddenly on the floor, unable to speak, and my eyes closed briefly. The woman who led the tour seemed very upset, and she gave me two extra souvenirs, so that I had three different little dolls, each locked in its own plastic brooch, that I could wear on my shirt. They had different color hair, pink, green, and purple, and were scented like flowers, each no taller than my thumb.

The gift didn't have the desired effect; I thrust the little dolls away and had what was later described as hysterics. My grandmother's payment for the last three weeks of camp was refunded, and she was asked that I not return. Mother, for her part, was quite disgusted with me, and the nicest thing she said was that at least the camp had kept me longer than the swimming school.

BARBIE DOLL

Patricia Storace

I

Her body, which is perfect,
is impenetrable.
It is her capsule,
orbiting
through childhoods which follow
childhoods which follow
childhoods,
the nest of decades
that emerge from one another.
Children are her oxygen.
The life oils in their hands
have made her plastic
tougher than muscle or bone.
The one way to destroy her
is dismemberment.
Her perfection is a violence.
Fling her to the soil;
she stands upright and
quivers, a thrown knife.
Grasp her carelessly,
her feet and hands
can damage, the flesh
laddered suddenly with blood.
One of the small things
that cause consequences;
a slap, a razor,
a pinch of cyanide.

One of the things
whose smallness is a honing;
a piranha,
the switchblade of the ocean.

II

The waist is rigid as a doctrine,
the body formed to carry clothes,
the feet shaped to stiletto heels,
frozen into point, the toes.

Marked with factory signature,
yields to credit or to cash,
made not to caress, but pose;
modeled for a camera flash.

The fingers durable and plastic
webbed together, form a hand,
the third emerges like a thorn,
soliciting a wedding band.

The detail royal on all the gowns
pearls sugaring the wedding dress,
a perfect doll, unbreakable;
stony and nippleless, the breasts.

TWELVE-STEP BARBIE

Richard Grayson

1. Van Nuys Barbie

Passing the window of a Judaica store in a strip shopping center on Victory Boulevard, she catches her reflection and instinctively begins to turn her head. But no! this time she will stop and look. Behind the oversized dark glasses she peers at the woman in the tangerine jogging suit with pink fuzzy trim. Barbie frowns.

What a disaster.

The young Latino boys coming out of the health food store don't even see her, or if they do, they think she's some housewife looking at kiddush cups and books about the Holy Land.

The nausea she vaguely feels is probably hunger, she decides, and she heads for the McDonald's at the corner. She knows she probably should go home and fix herself a salad, but she'll order the garden salad at Mickey D's. And the McLean Deluxe.

But when the perky black teenager at the counter asks, "May I take your order?" she finds herself saying:

"Big Mac, small fries, large Diet Coke."

2. Small Businesswoman Barbie

She's tried to dress for the interview with the loan officer. Everything hurt when she got up at 5 A.M. Barbie tried those stretches recommended by Amy, the blond exercise leader on the "Homestretch" TV show, but they didn't help much. Barbie exercises only at home now; she won't go to the health club anymore. She likes Amy because Amy seems down-to-earth, says never do more than you can do without pain, has a bad shoulder herself. It's the two women on the raised row behind Amy she hates: the perfect ones, even if they say they've had two children. When they do bench step exercises on "Homestretch," Barbie uses a scale because she hasn't gotten around to buying a bench step yet.

The loan officer at the Takemishuga Bank has been dealing with her for two years now, ever since she and her partner started the asbestos-removal business, but the man never seems to remember Barbie's name.

He has to look for it on the application form for the new loan. The loan officer is about twenty-seven, a redhead with freckles. Barbie notices a wedding band on his left hand, a photo of a pretty blond woman on his desk. The kind of guy who would have memorized not only her name but her face and every inch of her body in the past.

But today the talk is credit crunch, amortization, and asbestos. He'll let her know, she hears as they shake hands. He tries to be hopeful:

"At least you've found a niche: cleaning up dangerous messes."

Barbie smiles for the first time that morning.

3. Dysfunctional Barbie

Every time Skipper calls, all Barbie hears is how much pain she's in. Skipper was never as strong as Barbie. Barbie was the good child, the older sister who knew everything. Now that she and Skipper were in the same boat, Barbie hated having to comfort her all the time, give her advice, jolly her along through another day.

She never thinks to ask me about my symptoms, Barbie thinks as Skipper's sobs reach the 818 area code.

4. Sun-Block Barbie

In the shower, she feels that tingle in the middle of her back, in the place she can't reach. The little scar there is the least of her problems these days, but she wonders why there's that tingle when water hits it sometimes.

The dermatologist told her it was unrelated to her immune system problems. No, the little basal cell carcinoma was common for L.A. kids like herself who'd spent so much time at Zuma Beach. She didn't tell him about Island Fun Barbie. The sun was the same, Barbie knew, in Southern California as in the Caribbean, but she blamed the tiny cancer on what she thought of as the "foreign" sun.

Today she'll pull her hair—at least that's still pretty good—back in a ponytail. Barbie will use a rubber band, not her old pink skirt that doubled as a ponytail holder. She uses that when she cleans the Toyota now.

5. One-Day-at-a-Time Barbie

In the smoky room Barbie holds the sweaty hands of two other people as they stand up and pulse: "Keep coming back, it works if you work it." And then what would be the usual sigh if the AA meeting were a person.

She prefers the people at this Burbank church to the nonsmokers who meet on Tuesdays in the Presbyterian church closer to her house. Too many people know who she was there. Barbie's better off coming home with the smell of cigarettes on her clothes. She remembers not to wear her good clothes to the Burbank church meetings.

6. Laissez-Faire Barbie

Midge and Allan are arguing again. Barbie hates when they go out to a restaurant and do that. Midge is so petty sometimes, argues just to see how much Allan will take before exploding. Barbie wonders if Allan ever hit Midge. She looks down at her calamari and doubts it.

Barbie takes a sip of water and thinks about the burn Midge had on her cheek last month. It was probably just what Midge said: that problem with the hibachi. Still. She sips more water.

Despite all the recent rain, the storms didn't get up north, where the reservoirs are. Barbie tries to be good about conserving water, but even though she lives by herself, she can't bear the thought of not flushing the toilet after each time.

Midge gives Allan a look that says, You're embarrassing me in front of our friends again.

Barbie couldn't care less.

7. Bilingual Barbie

Barbie is talking to a health education class in a Long Beach high school. Scooter got her started doing that a few months ago, and while Barbie was reluctant at first, she found that she enjoyed the experience. It wasn't the kind of attention she got as Style Magic Barbie or California Dream Barbie, but she liked seeing the faces of the sixteen-year-old girls, so different from the face she had once seen in the mirror of her old fluorescent vanity.

The faces of the girls in this class are mostly Mexican and Cambodian. The teacher told her that several of the girls already have babies. Barbie once did a whole talk in Spanish for a class in East L.A., but here she talks in English, without the uhms and ahhs that used to punctuate her speech. She still says "like" more than she'd like. Still, that makes her more believable to these girls.

A Cambodian girl asks her about condoms, and Barbie's mind flashes back to Ken. With Ken, of course, condoms were never an issue.

Barbie answers all the questions, even the personal ones about what her body looks like now. As the bell rings, the health education class applauds Barbie, and a group of Mexican girls ask Barbie to sign the back of their jackets.

8. Reflective Barbie

Driving back from Long Beach, Barbie feels so good about the appearance at the high school, she doesn't notice the pains in her fingers. She has the radio on but doesn't hear Shadow Traffic telling her about the five-car accident on the Hollywood Freeway by Universal Studios, so she gets stuck in the middle lane. Her mind wanders.

Shutting off the all-news station when she hears the same story about canceling the Japanese rail cars for the third time, Barbie pops on the tape player. Expecting to hear Billy Joel, she gets Public Enemy instead. Yesterday her cousin Jazzy's rad boyfriend Dude borrowed the car; she lets him help out on the asbestos-removal jobs after school. Barbie is about to shut off the rap music but she discovers, when she can make out the words, that the lyrics make a lot of sense.

"Nine-one-one is a joke," raps Chuck D.

Damn right, Barbie thinks. Once again the picture of Ken pops into her head. In the old days she would josh Ken by calling him "Hardhead" because his hair wouldn't move, unlike her own thick, lustrous mane. For a a couple of years in the early seventies, he tried being Mod Hair Ken, but it didn't suit him and he returned to his former style. Ken learned to laugh when Barbie called him Hardhead. It wasn't the part of his body that was really the problem.

9. Bill-Paying Barbie

At her desk, Barbie listens to her pet tropical bird make its odd sound. Not a coo, not a chirp, a sort of sick sound. She got rid of most of her old things, but she couldn't bear to part with the bird with its reversible two-color wings. The Mattel people never should have done that to that bird. In her checkbook register are several checks made out to Friends of Animals.

Writing out a minimum payment on her I. Magnin bill, Barbie wonders if the bird with the artificial reversible wings also had a suppressed immune system.

10. Pissed-Off Barbie

When Skipper whines again about how bad she has it, Barbie finally loses it.

She laces into Skipper, bringing up things from the past, things better left unsaid. Skipper is shocked into silence.

Later the sisters talk, really talk for the first time in years, over Red Zinger tea and Entenmann's fat-free Louisiana crunch cake.

"You'd think our both getting sick would have made us closer," Barbie said, "but in a way I think it's, I don't know . . ."

Skipper nods. "Yeah, I've been a pain in the ass."

Barbie smiles. It isn't the perky smile or the come-hither smile or the smile on the face of Fun to Dress Barbie in the old days. "Yeah," Barbie says. "I should have told you before."

Skipper nods again. And Barbie talks about the Cambodian high school girls in Long Beach and what their parents must have gone through when the killing fields were going on. Barbie rented the movie three times. She couldn't understand how she missed the Cambodian holocaust when it was going on, but in those days she was Young Republican Barbie and she supported President Nixon on the war.

As Barbie sees Skipper to the door, gives her a hug, in her office there's a fax coming in from her lawyer.

11. Litigious Barbie

She didn't really mind coming out as the leading plaintiff in the class-action suit. Most of the publicity was favorable, although somebody in Dow Corning's high command tried to accuse her of constantly suing people back in the old days. It just wasn't true.

Yes, there was the problem with those Taiwanese knockoffs, but it was just that—and that messy business with Babette. It was so unpleasant, really, but they told her that even if they couldn't meet the demand for Barbie, they weren't going to let Babette take away any business.

The worst part was when they put Babette on the witness stand and she completely went to pieces under the harsh cross-examination by Mattel's lawyer. "Who'd confuse us?!" Babette finally screamed, and she startled the courtroom by removing her sweater and bra, and pointing to her pathetic little chest, kept saying over and over, "Who'd confuse us?"

Coming out of the courthouse, the press photographers' cameras were not aimed at Barbie's face but her bustline.

Barbie won the lawsuit, of course, and Babette slipped into obscurity. Now Barbie wishes she had handled Babette differently.

Thinking of her life as a stewardess, registered nurse, skin diver, fashion editor, and astronaut, Barbie knows she should have handled a lot of things differently. Especially Ken.

12. Twelve-Step Barbie

Ironically, it was the suit about the silicone implants that reunited her with Ken. He was Kendra now, a fellow plantiff. Skipper had met her (him?) at a new support group meeting that Barbie couldn't get to. Kendra told Skipper that despite the arthritis and the deformity and all the other auto-immune problems, she was happier now than when he was a man without a penis. After he disappeared from Barbie's life so suddenly, he became Gender Reassignment Ken and finally Kendra with the same artificial breasts that gave Barbie and Skipper and others all those problems.

Barbie and Kendra had brunch at the Boulangerie in Santa Monica, where real birds, none with reversible two-color wings, flew inside freely. After an initial awkwardness, they rediscovered what they liked about each other, what they had missed the first time.

BARBIE DOLLS

Leslie Shiel

I

Camille had more Barbies
than anyone on the block.
Her sisters, Danette and Alexis,
chewed on the feet of each new Barbie,
and when they were chewed off,
Camille screwed off the heads
and threw them in a box
with all the other Barbies
who had lost to Danette and Alexis.

When I tired of my Barbie,
the one with the red-bubble cut
my mother liked,
I popped off its head and traded it
for one of Camille's.

II

Camille had all the equipment:
beach houses and studio apartments.
She wrapped the dresses to much bigger dolls
round and round her Barbies,
tying them with shoe laces at the waists.

At my house, we played Barbies
outside on the porch,
used a cake pan for a swimming pool
and tied the red-bubble Barbie
to the back of a dachshund.

III

Camille's Barbies always took care
of Camille's Kens. Long-haired Barbies
wrapped in Camelot dresses, bent over
soldier Kens shot down in alleys, lying
in ditches. My Barbies were tired.
They just wanted to have fun with the Kens.

IV

One day for kindergarten
I wore the red dress from Grandmother
    Pettit
and ran out of the house
forgetting something for show and tell.

It was the first day to cross
the street by myself, to meet Camille
who brought a spider, to walk
the whole mile to Southridge School.

The red dress had big pockets.
My mother called from far away.
I ran back. She stuck
the red-bubble Barbie in my pocket.

V

In my room, on a Sunday afternoon,
King Kong attacked the red-bubble Barbie.
The air outside was gray.
My parents talked in the living room.
They faced off on the pillows, Barbie
in my right hand, the gorilla in my left.

VI

In eighth grade, Camille and I
had Guidance Class together:
all girls and Mr. H.
Once, we put our noses
to the floor because we had brown eyes
and he had blue and it was a lesson
in prejudice. Under her breath,
Camille swore to have her rights,
but I just watched a spider
stagger across the white-tiled floor.

And one day, he leaned into his podium
bulldoglike, and said, *Barbies are bad
because they have big boobs.*

No. That is not why
Barbies are bad. Barbies are bad
because their bodies are not their own.

FROM

THAT NIGHT

Alice McDermott

heryl called hi to me from the sidewalk in front of our house and then to my surprise and delight walked up our driveway. She carried her looseleaf binder and a small paperback book. There was a dark, pilly sweater thrown over her arm.

This was in the early spring, four months or so before that night. It had been a warm day, perhaps the first warm day of the season, and although it was now growing cool, there was still the lingering odor of bright sunlight, the spring smell of fresh dirt. I had brought my Barbie doll out to the front porch, probably because my brother and his friends were somewhere in the house and this was my way of showing my disdain. I had the black dollcase opened at the top of the steps and was choosing a dinner outfit.

Sheryl said as she approached, "How are you?" as if she asked quite regularly.

I must have said something like "Fine."

"This your Barbie?" she asked.

I said yes.

"It's nice." She suddenly sat on the step just below mine and placed her books on her lap. I could see the initials she had written all over her looseleaf binder with black magic marker, hers and Rick's. I noticed how the ink had bled a little into the fabric. I could have been glimpsing her garter belt, her diary, the initials seemed so adult and exotic, so indicative of everything I didn't know.

Turning a little, she reached back to my dollcase and

gently touched all the tiny dresses and skirts that were hanging there. Her fingers were thin and short and the edges of her nails pressed into her flesh as if she had only recently stopped chewing them. Then she touched the bare feet of the doll.

"She needs shoes," she said.

I told her I was trying to decide which outfit to put on.

Sheryl looked through the clothes again and extracted a pale blue jumper with a white frilly blouse.

"This is cute," she said.

I'd had something more sophisticated in mind, but I was somewhat bewildered by her presence—did she really want to play?—and so I bowed to what I thought was her better judgment.

I slipped off the brown sheath the doll was wearing. (Someday I'll do a study: What's become of that part of my generation who insisted that their Barbie dolls wear underpants and bras? What's become of the rest of us, who dressed her only in what could be seen?)

"Where's she going?" Sheryl asked.

"Out to dinner," I said.

Sheryl held the dress by its little hanger. "On a date?"

I nodded.

"With her boyfriend?"

I said, "Yeah." At that age I was suspicious of any adult, any teenager, who too willingly joined in my imaginary games. But Sheryl was good. There was no smirk behind her words.

"Well then," she said, "you want something dressier than this." She again looked through the clothes and this time extracted a strapless red dress with a wide gold lamé belt. It was the dress I had more or less planned to choose from the start.

As I slipped the naked doll into it, Sheryl opened her purse and began to rummage through it. There was a sound of tumbling and clicking, plastic and glass.

"Do you have a boyfriend?" she asked me.

I said I didn't.

"Not even anyone you like a little bit?"

I shook my head. I wasn't saying. "Where's your boyfriend?" I asked her.

She looked up from her bag and glanced toward her house. "He had to go to the hospital to pick up his mother," she said. "She's been sick, she's a nut case, but now she's coming home. For a while anyway, the weekend. He's got to help out." She lifted her black bag again and squinted into it. "I guess I won't see him until tomorrow or something."

I understood: she was bored, friendless, without him. She was speaking to me merely to pass the time, maybe to keep from having to go home.

I watched her extract a single cigarette and a match-book from her bag. She looked at me cautiously but without a word and then lit up. I watched her draw, her chin raised.

"Are you going steady?" I asked, although I knew.

She said, "Yeah," smoke pouring from her nostrils, and then lifted her arm to show me Rick's heavy ID bracelet. She turned her wrist to show me where she'd had a jeweler add an extra catch so it wouldn't slip over her hand. The inside of her wrist was pale white, almost blue, marked with red and purple veins. She pulled the bracelet around so the nameplate rested there. We both looked at it. The name was engraved in bold straight lines like Roman numerals.

I leaned over my lap to touch it and was surprised to find it wasn't ice-cold.

"Did he have to ask you?" I said, making plans of my own. "Did you have to wait until he asked you to go steady?"

"He had to ask me," she said. She turned the bracelet again and then shook her wrist until it fell, just so, over the back of her hand. "But I knew he was going to." She looked at me from under her bangs. "I knew it the minute I met him."

Her perfume reminded me of my father's after-shave. Her eyes were rimmed with smooth black eyeliner that grew, expertly, I thought, thick just over her eyeball and then quickly tapered to a fine, feathery tail that ended about a quarter of an inch beyond the corner of her eye. There was a touch of white powder on her lids.

"How did you know?" I asked.

She held the cigarette between the porch step and her legs and slowly leaned back against the railing. "I just knew," she said. She raised her other hand to brush the bangs from her eyes. The bracelet slid down her arm.

"But how?" I said again. "Who told you?"

Sheryl shrugged and then pulled her lips over her teeth to smile. "No one told me," she said. "I just knew it. In fact, I told him." She looked toward her house again. There were thin short wisps of hair pulled down in front of her ears like sideburns. There was something hard and tense about the set of her jaw. She quickly raised the cigarette. "I told him the very first night we met."

This was marvelous to me: that she knew, that she told him. And more, that she was here telling me.

"What did he say?" I asked her.

She toyed with the corner of her paperback, flipping the pages. "He didn't know," she said. She looked at me. "See, he'd had a lot of girlfriends before me. He didn't think it was going to be any different. He just kind of said, 'Oh yeah?'" She raised her chin, imitating him, then laughed again.

I was still leaning toward her, my Barbie doll all but forgotten. I don't think I'd ever been this close to Sheryl before—certainly not for this long—and I don't know which I took in more eagerly, what she said or how she looked. I remember there were a few pimples on her chin, almost buried beneath the thick makeup, a few flecks of pale pink lipstick on her small mouth. Her cigarette smoke curled toward me, and I breathed deeply.

"What we have," she said, and she may have looked a little sly as she spoke, "is completely different."

"How come?" I asked.

She thought for a moment and then leaned forward, pulling her books up onto her lap, her tight skirt binding her thighs. I saw the flash of her ankle bracelet under her dark stocking: another gift from Rick, another sign of going steady.

"It's just different," she said. She was holding her mouth as if she wanted to grin. "I mean, I'm not like any of those other girls. I've been through a lot of things and so I know more." She seemed to squint at me, perhaps gauging my understanding. "And I'm not afraid of anything," she added. "I'm really not."

I nodded. I saw that she had written their initials on the cover of her paperback as well.

"I'm not even afraid of dying," she told me, the cigarette at her lips. Her tone was pleasant but self-assured. She blew smoke upward into the air. "They showed us movies of these car accidents in school and it didn't even bother me. Even Rick got nervous when he saw them, but I said, 'So what? Everyone's going to die.'" She looked at me carefully through the smoke and then sat back again, letting her head touch the railing. She wore a navy-blue scarf around her throat. One end was thrown behind her, the other hung down in front of her bright red shell. Except for a small bruise just above her scarf, what the Meyer twins had taught us to recognize as a love bite, her throat was as white as the inside of her wrist.

"Pretty day," she said softly, looking up at the sky. I looked, too, ready to follow her anywhere. "Yeah," I said.

And then, still studying the sky, she told me, "My father died last year."

I don't know when the deaths in other people's lives stop seeming merely inevitable and start becoming a kind of embarrassment. I know that now I would greet such a statement with a quick consolation and a change of subject, but then I simply said, "I know it."

With her head still back, she turned and once again reached out to touch the doll dresses, the cigarette burning between her fingers. "Before that," she said with some disgust, "I didn't know anything. I thought it was stupid that people you really loved could just die. I used to think that it would be better if we were all like squirrels or something so when people died we wouldn't feel so terrible."

She dropped her hand and slowly ran her finger along the edge of the step. "I didn't know anything," she said.

Then she raised her head and looked at me. Her mouth was low in her face. There were clumps of mascara in her long lashes. "Listen," she said. "If you knew everybody you loved was just going to end up disappearing, you'd probably say, Why bother, right? You'd probably even stop liking people if you knew it wasn't going to make any difference, they're just going to eventually disappear. Right?" She leaned closer. I began to understand what my mother meant when she said that girls who dressed like Sheryl looked tough. There was something tough, even arrogant about her now. "I mean how logical is it," she went on, "for you to love somebody and then they just die, like you never existed? How stupid would it be to keep loving someone who was dead if you were never going to see them again—what do you love, then, air?"

I shrugged and she suddenly sat back. "No you don't," she said impatiently. "You don't end up loving air."

She raised her cigarette again, her elbow resting on the binder. "That's why it wouldn't matter if Rick got killed or something," she went on, cool, even nonchalant. "I guess it would be lonely, but it wouldn't be like I'd never see him again or anything. It would be just like with me and my father. I miss him, but I know I'm going to see him again because I think about him all the time. And you don't keep loving someone who doesn't exist anymore. You can't just stop loving someone because they die. Right?" She suddenly looked at me, demanding a response. "Right?"

"Right," I said softly. I had no idea what she was talking about. "I guess."

She glanced down at her books, ran her finger over the inked initials. "The problem with Rick was nobody loved him enough before me. If he had died, and once he was in a car accident where he could have, he wouldn't have had anyone who still cared about him. He would have just stopped being, like a squirrel or a cat or something. He would have been forgotten about completely. Maybe not right away, but eventually." She picked a piece of tobacco from her tongue, lowering her thick lashes as she did, and then flicked her cigarette, dropping ashes onto our bricks. "His mother has mental problems. Sometimes she even forgets about him now, so what difference would it make to her if he died all of a sudden? She's in her own world. I met her one time." She shook her head. "And his father has too many problems to ever really think about him. His sister, too. If he had died before he met me, everybody would have felt bad for a little while and then they would have forgotten about him. Pretty soon it would have been like he'd never been born in the first place. But I wouldn't forget."

We sat silently for a few minutes. My backside was growing cold against the bricks, but I didn't want to go inside.

"Are you getting married?" I asked her.

She shrugged and again looked over her shoulder to

her own house before snuffing out her cigarette and tossing it onto our lawn. "I guess so," she said. She leaned back once more, holding an elbow in each palm. She was completely, amazingly, self-possessed. Completely sure. Tough.

"Probably we'll get married," she said. It was clear the subject was not nearly as interesting to her as their immortality. "Maybe in a couple of years. Not that it would make any difference." She glanced at me, but I failed to catch her meaning. "None of that matters to us. You know, getting married and having kids and buying a house. None of that means anything to us."

"How come?" I asked, and she smiled as if she had just proven her point.

"I told you," she said. "I know things. I've been through things. I know all those things that other people think are important come down to nothing. They disappear."

The air had grown chillier, but it was a spring chill, without the bite of winter. Sheryl suddenly arched her back and reached up to touch the teased crown of her hair. There were a thousand things I wanted to ask her: what movies she and Rick went to, what she said to him when he called her on the phone, when they sat together in his car—how she drew such perfect lines across her eyelids.

The death stuff amazed me, but no more than all the rest. It seemed only a part, a profound, important but no less puzzling part of all I would need to know in order to become a teenager. All that I feared I would somehow fail to learn.

Sheryl lifted the Barbie doll from my lap, adjusted her belt and hair, turned to the dollcase to find a pair of little red high heels. I wished she were my sister and I wondered without much hope if she could somehow become my friend. She handed the doll back to me and suggested I wrap a white stole around her bare shoulders.

As I buttoned the tiny fur, I said, "Well, I hope Rick doesn't die."

"Everybody's going to die," she said quickly, and I thought for certain that I'd completely missed her point. Then she smiled, nodding slightly. "But I know what you mean," she said.

She gathered her books into her arms. I watched her walk home: the clink of his bracelet, the gold flash from her ankle, the paperback and looseleaf binder marked with their names. There was something sullen about her walk, a kind of challenge. I saw her toss her hair back over her shoulder before she pulled open the front door, armed and ready, it seemed to me, to battle even the Angel of Death.

EXPERIENCE

Laura Costas

arbie said, Go climb trees. She said, Run fast, honey, swagger, curse. You don't want to be like me, pinched and pointed and curled.

She said, Be a Jet, go ahead. Wear glasses, mumble, and spit. Don't be fooled, Barbie said, let me tell you, this professional life is a drag.

I know I look nice. I'm what everyone wants; I'm fulfillment, confection, art. But Barbie said, You don't want it, just trust me. Hold out, make them guess, break their hearts.

Don't envy me my ornaments, Barbie said. Forget matching luggage, the sports car, and Ken. Travel light, little sister, why gild a lily? Try white ankle socks and some sensible shoes.

If I could, Barbie said, I'd ditch this name, this prickly, blood-drawing boundary of sound. For you I see prairies, go with Amanda, Susan, Irene.

Oh please, Barbie said, Don't you mention my martyred hair. I denounce this lacquered, preternatural lid. Wear goofy bangs, get a crewcut, devolve. Be Salome instead.

And spread out, Barbie said. Why go through life shaped like a railroad spike? Use your elbows, make shade, take up space.

I seem in the pink, don't I, sweetheart? Barbie said, It's true, but perfection is tough. Tonsillitis is out, I won't be excused, I can't apologize for the mess. Do it your way, she said, make a date with the mumps, trash your room, come undone.

I'm rectitude's right hand, but, Barbie said, who loves

the absolute? Blur the edges girlfriend, go on, let it go. Be fugitive, indifferent, obscure.

I'm sad, Barbie said, sad and smiling, smiling and sad. I'm a mental-health squeeze play, don't try this at home. You make them love the loser in you, go chew on a toothpick and sulk.

Look, Barbie said, Don't you see who I am? I expect nothing from you, you'll get nothing from me. I'm iron, infertile, complete. It's too late for me, but you, you're still young, play Hamlet, bet the farm, tell the truth.

I say, Thanks, Barbie.

VOODOO SILENCES

Sharon Henry

Barbie could talk. For a little while, at least. Pull the pink plastic daisy ring at the back of her long neck and all those words came tumbling out. Even my big sister doesn't have a talking Barbie.

"Hi! I'm Barbie. Will you be my . . . Will you be my . . . Will you . . . you . . ."

She used to ask, "Will you be my friend?" but now she's just getting stuck and choking on her words. Holding her like a wounded bird in my arms, I run down the hall. Crashing down the staircase, blind with new tears, and into the musty downstairs and then the garage. "It's all right. It's all right." I'm promising myself as much as I'm promising to Barbie. "It's going to be okay. Daddy can fix anything."

Dad's hunched over his workbench, soldering something on a fuseboard. I can smell the hot metal. I burned myself with that once, but he put one of the special Band-Aids from the first aid kit on it. It left that long pink scar line on the back of my thumb. Finally, when I sniffle, he looks up from his work. Didn't even hear me coming through the door. "What's wrong now?"

He's not patient with me anymore. And I don't know why. It's just how it is now. I hold Barbie out in front of me and pull the string in her neck.

"Hi. I'm Barbie. Can I be your . . . Can I . . . Can I . . ."

He doesn't even turn off the soldering iron. Just moves it to the side. Reaches out to take her away from me, turns her over and looks at her back, covered with tiny holes where the sound comes out. I stand and want to watch this, want to see what he's going to do to her.

"Tina. Why don't you go upstairs and ask your mother to take you to the park, okay?"

I don't want to go, but I know when I've been dismissed. Not welcome down here anymore. Didn't used to be like this.

I used to sit there on the edge of his workbench for hours at a time, watching him fix things. Mom would have to come down to scoot me upstairs to help in the kitchen. I'd plead to stay for just a little longer, looking up at her with my best smile, thinking I must look like a little bird. "Look, Mommy. Daddy can do anything!"

"Yeah. Okay. Come on, honey. Let's go upstairs and get you cleaned up. You're filthy. Like a little dog. Don't know why your father lets you get into a mess like this."

But I wear dresses now, and I don't like the smells anymore— damp newspapers, gasoline, paint, and the dust. I play upstairs now, like my sister Jenn. I play with Barbie when Jenn won't let me play with her and her friends because I'm still too little. But he never used to tell me I was too little. I was his assistant. I'd hold the clamps for him, or sort all the screws and nails into neat little plastic drawers, or be a nurse when he operated, and ask a thousand questions.

"You talk a lot, Tina. If you do that, the boys won't like you." Grandma always tells me that, but I don't care. I'm only eight, and the only boy I care about is Ken. And he can't talk, so I have to do all the talking for him.

Barbie's head won't go back on. Her torso's been split in half. The sad little plastic daisy hanging useless and wilted on its string. Her magic voice a teeny-tiny record in her back. All the king's horses and all the king's men, even Daddy, can't put her together again. I just stare at Barbie's silent broken parts lying on the kitchen table.

Mom and Dad are screaming at each other in her bedroom.

"So what! I'll buy her a new one."

"Well, you'd better. You just had to see how it worked,

didn't you? Didn't even think about that little girl out there. That's her *doll*, for God's sake. Do you have any idea what that means?"

It's been a month. Still no new Barbie. I'm locked in my room, so no one can bother me, no one can interrupt this world I'm making. Have to use my Malibu Barbie as the heroine in this story because Talking Barbie's dead. Besides, *she* wasn't usually in these games. She talked to me. Like a pet bird. These silent ones work better for stories because then I make it all up myself. Put all the words into their plastically sealed mouths. They work better like that, you know.

"Tina! Tina, Where are you?"
　　He's all the way downstairs in his room. I can't interrupt the game at this moment. Ken and Barbie have just agreed to get married and now they are pressed as closely together as their rigid plastic bodies will allow. "TINA!"
　　"In a minute."
　　"Tina. You come down here this instant."
　　Mom's out at the grocery store shopping and Jenn is watching a movie on TV. No one to intervene. But this is the most important part of the game! This is what all the two hours of dressing and undressing have been leading to. If I leave now, I ruin it.
　　"Not right now! I'm busy."
　　"Christina Marie. Don't you dare talk back to me! Get yourself down here right now before I come up there!"
　　That's it. Game's over.

"Tina, have you been playing with my tape recorder again?"
　　He's holding it out in front of him, right under my nose. I'm shaking 'cause I know. Know I didn't put it back where he left it and now he knows I didn't ask for permission.
　　"No."
　　"Don't lie. Tina, how many times have I told you, you have to ask to use this."
　　There's a twitch in the side of his cheek. I've seen him grind his teeth before, but not like this. Never like this. "I put it back. Really, I did."
　　"Listen to this!"

A strangled sound, choking like my Barbie did, comes out.

"I didn't break it. I didn't! It was fine when I put it back. Jenn must have been playing tapes on it. I swear, it was fine."

"Don't you lie to me again, Christina!"

"But I'm not lying!" I'm crying.

"I'll teach you not to talk back to me!"

The blows are coming so fast. Like he's an octopus and I'm a little boat in his grasp. His face isn't even his own anymore. Like one of those dog-lions in front of the Chinese restaurant. I know I'm screaming because I see Jenn standing frozen stiff on the stairs, covering her ears but too scared to look away. I'm going to die. Just let go, and the storm will take me down. My free hand finds his face. He's too busy trying to drive the life out of me to push it away. First the glasses go, knocked away. Two fingers smooshed together find the slippery softness of his eye. He roars backward in pain. I run faster than my heart can drum, up the stairs, past the statue of Jennifer, into my room. Barricade the door with everything I own till Mom comes home.

Under the covers, I lie completely still. The sheets keep out the light, but everywhere I'm touched it stings. My arms already too swollen to bend. They lie like plastic Barbie arms, stiff at my sides. A teddy bear at each hand so I can touch them even though I can't hold them.

"Daddy can fix anything. Daddy can fix anything. Daddy can fix . . . Daddy can . . . Daddy can . . . Daddy can fix . . . you."

BARBIE MEETS THE SCARIEST FATSO YET

Cookie Lupton

So Barbie's depressed,
and it's January,
the second semester
of her sophomore year at State U.
She goes to get help
for starving herself,
plunks her name on the waiting list
and wonders how to break the news:
Sometimes I don't eat.
Sometimes I puke.
I feel like hell, so fix it.

Ten pounds mean the world,
and Barbie chews her tongue
like a wad of unnecessary fat
because all fat is bad and
belongs in the basement.
She feels dank and musty,
like mildew from an overripe June in '71
that's locked in a trunk
with sweaters and mothballs and old cat glasses,
and that's when he walks out:
Freddy Doolittle, Ph.D.,
400 pounds of polyester plaid
with a shredded carrot skullcap
and a light blue oxygen face.

PLAYING WITH DOLLS

David Trinidad

Every weekend morning, I'd sneak downstairs to play
with my sisters' Barbie dolls. They had all
of them: Barbie, Ken, Allan, Midge, Skipper, and
Skooter. They even had the little freckled boy,
Ricky ("Skipper's Friend"), and Francie, "Barbie's
'MOD'ern cousin." Quietly, I'd set the dolls

in front of their wardrobe cases, take the dolls'
clothes off miniature plastic hangers, and play
until my father woke up. There were several Barbies—
blond ponytail, black bubble, brunette flip—all
with the same pointed tits, which (odd for a boy)
didn't interest me as much as the dresses and

accessories. I'd finger each glove and hat and
necklace and high heel, then put them on the dolls.
Then I'd invent elaborate stories. A "creative" boy,
I could entertain myself for hours. I liked to play
secretly like that, though I often got caught. All
my father's tirades ("Boys don't play with Barbies!

It isn't *normal*!") faded as I slipped Barbie's
perfect figure into her stunning ice blue and
sea green satin and tulle formal gown. All
her outfits had names like "Fab Fashion," "Doll's
Dream," and "Golden Evening"; Ken's were called "Play
Ball!" "Tennis Pro," "Campus Hero," and "Fountain
    Boy,"

which came with two tiny sodas and spoons. Model boy
that he was, Ken hunted, fished, hit home runs. Barbie's
world revolved around garden parties, dances, play
and movie dates. A girl with bracelets and scarves and
sunglasses and fur stoles . . . "Boys don't play with dolls!"
My parents were arguing in the living room. "All

boys do." As always, my mother defended me. "All
sissies!" snarled my father. "He's a creative boy,"
my mother responded. I stuffed all the dresses and dolls
and shoes back into the black cases that said "Barbie's
Wonderful World" in swirling pink letters and
clasped them shut. My sisters, awake now, wanted to play

with me. "I can't play," I said, "Dad's upset." All
day, he stayed upset. Finally, my mother came upstairs
          and said: "You're a boy,
David. Forget about Barbies. Stop playing with dolls."

LIVING DOLL

FOR SHEREE LEVIN

David Trinidad

*T*he night we met, I was wearing one of my most ex-
quisite ensembles: formal, floor-length gown with
flowing train (in the elegance of pink satin), pearl necklace and drop earrings, pink dancing pumps with silver
glitter, white elbow gloves and fur stole. An enchanted evening! I can still hear those distant harps and violins, can
still recall how the laughter and chatter of the other guests
magically dissolved as we sipped champagne on the lush,
moonlit terrace. "He's such a doll!" I thought. "This must be
love at first sight!" Right then, I decided I wanted to spend
the rest of my days gazing into that dreamboat's blue eyes.

The following Sunday, Ken picked me up for a drive in the
country. I took the high-fashion road with my beige sweater
and striped pants, a car coat fastened with toggles, a straw
hat that ties with a red scarf, and wedgies to match . . . perfect
for a lunch stop in a picturesque village. Before I slid into the
passenger seat, I noticed the license plate on Ken's sports car.
It said MATTEL. I later learned he was the youngest and
fastest-rising executive the company had ever employed.

At that point, I was a little bewildered about the direction of
my own future. My modeling career seemed to be going nowhere. The photo sessions, fan mail, and fashion shows that
had once brought me fame were tapering off. I simply wasn't
up for it anymore. (It isn't easy being a teenage model at
twenty-five!) Besides, I wanted to do something different. Oh,
I had tried just about everything. As a ballerina, I danced

before kings and queens as the Sugar Plum Fairy, costumed in a shimmering silver tutu. As a stewardess, I took off for sky adventures in a navy blue uniform with flight insignia on cap and jacket. I'd even been a registered nurse and cured patients in my trim white uniform and silk-lined cape. Before I met Ken, I had been toying with the idea of pursuing a singing career. Although I'd started to appear at some of the nightclubs around town, I could tell this endeavor would never really get off the ground. The feelings I found myself developing for Ken gave my life new meaning, a definite direction. He seemed to fix it for me.

The next couple of months, we were practically inseparable. We went sailing and ice-skating. We played tennis at an exclusive country club. On our alpine holiday, I sported a swaggering leather coat, a striped T-shirt with jaunty hood, and knit mittens. Often, after cocktails, I twirled on dance floors in a feminine flower print accented with a fancy sash or a powder blue corduroy jumper with colorful felt appliqués and bouffant petticoat. For a garden party, I cultivated a cotton candy look: rosebuds, ruffles, and dainty pink bow at waist. I blossomed out for a fund-raising banquet in a buttercup yellow sheath frosted with sheer overskirt, smart hat, and a bouquet of spring posies to complete the pretty picture. But did Ken notice? Was it my imagination, or was he growing more and more remote?

I sensed something was amiss the night I debuted my new act at The Pink Lady Lounge. Didn't Ken realize what an important event it was? There were no tasteful floral arrangements, no expensive chocolates or vintage wines. I'd spent hours at the dressing room vanity in a frenzy of false eyelashes, mascara, powder puffs, lipsticks, and bobby pins. And still I didn't look right! I was completely beside myself. I'd misplaced one of my gold hoop earrings. I couldn't get the ribbon tied around my ponytail. I could barely fasten my bead necklace. At the last minute, I managed to slip into my dramatic black glitter-gown, the one with bare shoulders and a rose corsage on its netted flounce. I pulled on my long black gloves just as a stagehand ushered me into the wings . . . and before I knew it, I was standing at the microphone, in the middle of my first number, pink scarf in hand. Beyond the glare of the spotlight, I recognized a couple at one of the front tables. It was Allen and Midge. But where was Ken? I nearly collapsed several times during my performance. Afterwards, I kept the bartender company until last call, then took a taxi home.

What went wrong? Why won't he answer my messages? Whenever I phone his office, the curt receptionist says he's either in a conference or at the gym. Why won't he let me get close to him? Lately, all I do is mope around my apartment in a yellow terry cloth robe (with a big monogrammed *B* on the breast pocket). I oversleep and keep the drapes drawn all day. I'm gaining weight. There are dark circles under my eyes. I should try to pull myself together, but what about the plans we made? What about my Dream House and its complete suite of modern, slim-line furniture? What about my magnificent church wedding dress? It's fit for a princess: formal train, diamond tiara, tiered bridal veil, and billowing layers of flowered nylon tulle. What about my trousseau . . . my embroidered peignoir or my full-length pink negligee with its Grecian bodice and low-cut back? Are my dreams as flimsy? Are they as transparent as that?

HOW BARBIE WARPED ME

Lisa B. Herskovits

Barbie (the product) came into existence when I was a few years old. I was too little to have one of the first Barbies, but my older girlfriends on Noble Road in East Cleveland had those early models. Early Barbie had a blond ponytail, which curled frizzily at the ends. She had a sluttish, pouty face, torpedo tits, teeny, tiny little feet, and no hips at all. She looked like an alien from another planet, now that I think of it.

Soon enough, I had my first Barbie. She had short, red hair, styled into what my girlfriends (Cheryl and Claudia) called a "bubble do." You could get Barbies with or without earrings. Mine was without. Those earrings were scary. They were little gold blobs, on the ends of pieces of wire. You drove the wire spikes into Barbie's skull. I found it quite horrifying. I wondered why no one else thought this was bizarre. I figured I would understand it all when I "grew up." But those earrings really turned me off. To this day, my ears remain unpierced. I just couldn't go through with it—I'd remember Barbie, with those spikes being driven into her skull. And I'd put off getting my ears pierced.

My parents couldn't afford to buy me an extensive Barbie wardrobe, but I did have a shiny black patent leather carrying case for her, complete with a coffinlike section in which Barbie would reside, and little cardboard drawers and tiny plastic clothes hangers. My Barbie did have a nurse's outfit (I didn't like the white uniform dress, but I adored her cape) and a tight, black sequined evening dress, which came with a pink chiffon scarf, long gloves, and a microphone, so she could be a glamorous lounge singer. My Barbie also had some "generic" doll clothes, which weren't manufactured by Mattel. These included a white silk strapless brassiere, and nylon stockings (but no garter belt). (Mattel never produced underwear for Barbie. To get underwear for your Barbie, you had to turn to the "gray market.") She also had gray wool trousers, a couple of very cute orange sweaters, and casual sandals with cork wedge heels. Mine was a middle-class Barbie.

We had stationary tubs down in our basement, and I liked to fill them with water and make Barbie dive in. Her hairstyle was never ruined by the water, and her streamlined body dived beautifully, I thought, into the gray water, which, in my mind, was that of a glamorous outdoor swimming pool somewhere.

Cheryl and Claudia were two or three years older than I, and this made a pretty big difference, but they felt I was sometimes an acceptable playmate for them, nonetheless. ("Don't let them fondle you," my mother would warn, and I'd promise not to let them, but I'd always wonder what on Earth Mom was talking about!?) Cheryl, Claudia, and I would play "Barbies," usually down in Cheryl's basement.

There, her father set up a huge sheet of plywood on sawhorses, and this became the floor for the "apartment" we created for our Barbies, who all lived together and worked as waitresses in the same restaurant. At the end of our play sessions, we'd pretend it was nighttime, and our Barbies would go to "sleep," until we had a chance to play with them again. Sometimes we pretended it was night even when we didn't want to stop playing, and they'd call to each other, "Night . . . !" and they'd go to sleep for, perhaps, all of five seconds. Suddenly it would be morning, and they'd spring to life, like speed freaks, ready to take on a new day of waitressing to-gether.

We'd pick out names for our Barbies, but if we'd ever forget those names, we'd always call our dolls "Barbie," as if by default. Her identity—her persona—was built-in. You could always rely on Barbie to be . . . Barbie. Barbie aimed to please—you could make her be anyone, anything you wanted. She was pliable. Malleable. Indestructable.

I got a Ken doll. He had short yellow fuzz on his head.

We might have picked names for our Barbies, but Ken was always just "Ken."

Ken's wardrobe puzzled me. Why were there no bright colors? Why no frills, no lace? Why were his shoulders so much broader than Barbie's? Why on Earth wasn't he anatomically correct? I had seen Dad plenty of times, and I knew how Ken should—but didn't—look. I decided this was one of the many things I'd understand when I "grew up."

Barbie's body, too, puzzled me. Her hips were as slim as a boy's. I knew Real Women weren't like Barbie. Real Women had big, jiggly butts. Barbie, I decided, was some sort of "ideal" woman—a form to which we should all aspire. Barbie was Correct. We, the lowly Earthlings, were Not.

Barbie wore spike-heeled mules. To this day, no shoe looks right to me unless its heel is spiked. Barbie wore cat-glasses. So do I.

Of course, I could never get my makeup like Barbie's.

Whenever I ask my female friends about their child-hood Barbies, they always remember quite a bit. Their faces light up, and they talk animatedly about their beloved Barbies, and what type of persona they'd each been given. I came to realize that often, the persona each woman had given to her Barbie, as a child, was a carbon copy, albeit a simplified one, of the persona that little girl adopted as a grown woman.

For example, Cheryl's and Claudia's Barbies were boy-crazy. Cheryl and Claudia both grew up to be very convention-al-type women. My Barbie, on the other hand, was a rebel. She liked to put men down. She only dated them as a type of experiment. My Barbie liked to wear pants, and she also liked to wear a green satin evening dress to work as a waitress. She had lots of style, and never conformed to the boring rules of dress that everyone else had to.

There have been many strange Barbies and Barbie products over the years. One was Barbie's "dream house." My parents bought me one. Everything was made of card-board, and your parents would fold and assemble all the pieces, to make furniture, walls, and fixtures. The strangest Barbie product I ever saw came out in the mid-sixties. It was a Barbie head, with three wigs. You'd decapitate your "old" Barbie, and pop on a "new" head. The wigs were really strange. My favorite of the three had long, red hair, bangs in a sexy side part, and a "flip" at the end. I thought she looked like "Catwoman" in it.

Barbie had various female "friends." Midge was the first. I didn't care for Midge. She had red hair and freckles, and looked too much like my friend Cheryl for my comfort.

Later, came Francie. I got a Francie doll when I was almost too old for dolls. She had bendable legs. I figured out how to bend those legs and use them to pleasure myself.

Wherever Francie is, she probably still smells funny.

By the time I was a teenager, I found myself lusting after women, instead of men. After all, Barbie was a woman, and wasn't Barbie superior to Ken? Of course she was!

I would like to form Barbie Group Therapy groups. Bunches of women would meet for social, therapeutic "rap sessions"—fun ones, with champagne and hors d'oeuvres. We'd talk about our Barbies, and the personas we'd given them, as little girls. We'd discuss how we grew up, real-life versions of those Barbie-personae. There really is, I am certain, a strong correlation between the personalities of our childhood Barbies, and our personalities today.

But Barbie warped me. I am not right today, and it is largely because of Barbie.

It's all Barbie's fault.

Rather, it is the fault of those who created her. Didn't they know what they were doing to generations of females? Didn't they care?

Was this some sort of evil plot, to keep women down and confused?

And why didn't Barbie come with underwear?

THE BLACK LACE PANTIES TRIANGLE

Belinda Subraman

Ken had been looking for a Valentine's gift for his girlfriend, Barbie. When he saw a mannequin posed in a sexual position with an orgasmic expression on her face he knew exactly what he would give her. Black lace panties just like the ones on the dummy! It was almost like a sign from heaven, like something he'd always needed had been revealed to him. He could just imagine how Barbie would look and how he'd react. He could hardly wait to get them on her, and off her.

Barbie was delighted that Ken gave her a gift that would please them both. She felt a little selfish for just having given him a card. But she vowed to make up for it in her new black lace panties. She promised she wouldn't take them off until he was totally satisfied.

Ken reacted just as he knew he would. He ravished her in every position with his strapped-on cock. There was no need to remove the panties as the crotch was no more than a string that could be easily pushed aside.

Things got to be very intense at Barbie's apartment. Ken couldn't get enough and wouldn't allow Barbie to leave his side. When she went into the bathroom he followed her. While she brushed her teeth he entered her from behind. When she attempted to take a shower it only meant intercourse standing up with water as the background.

After fourteen straight hours of this, Barbie was sore and had all she could take. She told Ken she really needed to rest. But Ken only reminded her of her promise. He made her keep wearing the panties.

Barbie was not only sore and tired, by now she was also growing disgusted. Love had turned to pure lust and now lust was turning into abuse. He kept pushing himself on her until she had to yell, "Ken, this has gone far enough. Save some of it for the rest of your life. Don't spend it all in one day. Go home, Ken!"

But Ken dived for her crotch once more. Lust was like a growing cancer in him. Barbie managed to beat him to the bathroom and locked the door. She tore off the black panties, and threw them in the trash can. She then put on her robe from the back of the bathroom door and went out to her closet for some clothes.

As soon as Ken saw her, his face fell with disappointment, but he said nothing. He watched her dress and put on her makeup, but still he said nothing. Finally she got her purse and said, "Ken, I'm going out for a while. I want you to collect yourself then go back to your apartment and get some rest. When you feel like your old self again, give me a call."

Two hours later Barbie returned to find Ken gone. She halfway expected to find a note, but there wasn't one. She knew he'd call soon though. But he didn't, not that day or the next or ever.

Later when she went into the bathroom to take a shower she noticed that her black lace panties were gone too.

BARBIE'S CRANK CALL TO AN ESOTERIC TEMPLE

Belinda Subraman

O Grand Poo-Bah
of Egyptian Other Stupidness
why do your members
look retarded?
It's as if they said,
"If we had half a mind, we'd . . ."
and they did.
I look in the mirror.
I still see a genius.
I'm going to start a group
called Barbie-Crucians.
It will be more than platitudes
on slick paper. I'll make you
think. Every day you'll know
why you belong to me.
If you insist on initiation
I will get down
on my knees for you,
perform every rite.
There will be wetness
in your kundalini.
The aura of my karma
will transcend
your magic wandness.

Satori will come.
You will project it,
astrally speaking
into the mystery
of my burning bush.
NOT!

THE BARBIE MURDERS

John Varley

*T*he body came to the morgue at 2246 hours. No one paid much attention to it. It was a Saturday night, and the bodies were piling up like logs in a millpond. A harried attendant working her way down the row of stainless steel tables picked up the sheaf of papers that came with the body, peeling back the sheet over the face. She took a card from her pocket and scrawled on it, copying from the reports filed by the investigating officer and the hospital staff.

Ingraham, Leah Petrie. Female. Age: 35. Length: 2.1 meters. Mass: 59 kilograms. Dead on arrival, Crisium Emergency Terminal. Cause of death: homicide. Next of kin: unknown.

She wrapped the wire attached to the card around the left big toe, slid the deadweight from the table and onto the wheeled carrier, took it to cubicle 659A, and rolled out the long tray.

The door slammed shut, and the attendant placed the paperwork in the out tray, never noticing that, in his report, the investigating officer had not specified the sex of the corpse.

Lieutenant Anna-Louise Bach had moved into her new office three days ago and already the paper on her desk was threatening to avalanche onto the floor.

To call it an office was almost a perversion of the term. It had a file cabinet for pending cases; she could open it only at severe risk to life and limb. The drawers had a tendency to spring out at her, pinning her in her chair in the corner. To reach "A" she had to stand on her chair; "Z" required her either to sit on her desk or to straddle the bottom drawer with one foot in the leg well and the other against the wall.

But the office had a door. True, it could only be opened if no one was occupying the single chair in front of the desk.

Bach was in no mood to gripe. She loved the place. It was ten times better than the squad room, where she had spent ten years elbow to elbow with the other sergeants and corporals.

Jorge Weil stuck his head in the door.

"Hi. We're taking bids on a new case. What am I offered?"

"Put me down for half a Mark," Bach said, without looking up from the report she was writing. "Can't you see I'm busy?"

"Not as busy as you're going to be." Weil came in without an invitation and settled himself in the chair. Bach looked up, opened her mouth, then said nothing. She had the authority to order him to get his big feet out of her "cases completed" tray, but not the experience in exercising it. And she and Jorge had worked together for three years. Why should a stripe of gold paint on her shoulder change their relationship? She supposed the informality was Weil's way of saying he wouldn't let her promotion bother him as long as she didn't get snotty about it.

Weil deposited a folder on top of the teetering pile marked "For Immediate Action," then leaned back again. Bach eyed the stack of paper—and the circular file mounted in the wall not half a meter from it, leading to the incinerator—and thought about having an accident. Just a careless nudge with an elbow . . .

"Aren't you even going to open it?" Weil asked, sounding disappointed. "It's not every day I'm going to hand-deliver a case."

"You tell me about it, since you want to so badly."

"All right. We've got a body, which is cut up pretty bad. We've got the murder weapon, which is a knife. We've got thirteen eyewitnesses who can describe the killer, but we don't really need them since the murder was committed in front of a television camera. We've got the tape."

"You're talking about a case which has to have been

solved ten minutes after the first report, untouched by human hands. Give it to the computer, idiot." But she looked up. She didn't like the smell of it. "Why give it to me?"

"Because of the other thing we know. The scene of the crime. The murder was committed at the barbie colony."

"Oh, sweet Jesus."

The Temple of the Standardized Church in Luna was in the center of the Standardist Commune, Anytown, North Crisium. The best way to reach it, they found, was a local tube line which paralleled the Cross-Crisium Express Tube.

She and Weil checked out a blue-and-white police capsule with a priority sorting code and surrendered themselves to the New Dresden municipal transport system—the pill sorter, as the New Dresdenites called it. They were whisked through the precinct chute to the main nexus, where thousands of capsules were stacked awaiting a routing order to clear the computer. On the big conveyer which should have taken them to a holding cubby, they were snatched by a grapple—the cops called it the long arm of the law—and moved ahead to the multiple maws of the Cross-Crisium while people in other capsules glared at them. The capsule was inserted, and Bach and Weil were pressed hard into the backs of their seats.

In seconds they emerged from the tube and out onto the plain of Crisium, speeding along through the vacuum, magnetically suspended a few millimeters above the induction rail. Bach glanced up at the Earth, then stared out the window at the featureless landscape rushing by. She brooded.

It had taken a look at the map to convince her that the barbie colony was indeed in the New Dresden jurisdiction— a case of blatant gerrymandering if ever there was one. Anytown was fifty kilometers from what she thought of as the boundaries of New Dresden, but was joined to the city by a dotted line that represented a strip of land one meter wide.

A roar built up as they entered a tunnel and air was injected into the tube ahead of them. The car shook briefly as the shock wave built up, then they popped through pressure doors into the tube station of Anytown. The capsule doors hissed and they climbed out onto the platform.

The tube station at Anytown was primarily a loading dock and warehouse. It was a large space with plastic crates stacked against all the walls, and about fifty people working to load them into freight capsules.

Bach and Weil stood on the platform for a moment, uncertain where to go. The murder had happened at a spot not twenty meters in front of them, right here in the tube station.

"This place gives me the creeps," Weil volunteered.

"Me, too."

Every one of the fifty people Bach could see was identical to every other. All appeared to be female, though only faces, feet, and hands were visible, everything else concealed by loose white pajamas belted at the waist. They were all blond; all had hair cut off at the shoulder and parted in the middle, blue eyes, high foreheads, short noses, and small mouths.

The work slowly stopped as the barbies became aware of them. They eyed Bach and Weil suspiciously. Bach picked one at random and approached her.

"Who's in charge here?" she asked.

"We are," the barbie said. Bach took it to mean the woman herself, recalling something about barbies never using the singular pronoun.

"We're supposed to meet someone at the temple," she said. "How do we get there?"

"Through that doorway," the woman said. "It leads to Main Street. Follow the street to the temple. But you really should cover yourselves."

"Huh? What do you mean?" Bach was not aware of anything wrong with the way she and Weil were dressed. True, neither of them wore as much as the barbies did. Bach wore her usual blue nylon briefs in addition to a regulation uniform cap, arm and thigh bands, and cloth-soled slippers. Her weapon, communicator, and handcuffs were fastened to a leather equipment belt.

"Cover yourself," the barbie said, with a pained look. "You're flaunting your differentness. And you, with all that hair . . ." There were giggles and a few shouts from the other barbies.

"Police business," Weil snapped.

"Uh, yes," Bach said, feeling annoyed that the barbie had put her on the defensive. After all, this was New Dresden, it was a public thoroughfare—even though by tradition and usage a Standardist enclave—and they were entitled to dress as they wished.

Main Street was a narrow, mean little place. Bach had expected a promenade like those in the shopping districts of New Dresden; what she found was indistinguishable from a residential corridor. They drew curious stares and quite a few frowns from the identical people they met.

There was a modest plaza at the end of the street. It had a low roof of bare metal, a few trees, and a blocky stone building in the center of a radiating network of walks.

A barbie who looked just like all the others met them at the entrance. Bach asked if she was the one Weil had spoken to on the phone, and she said she was. Bach wanted to know if they could go inside to talk. The barbie said the temple was off limits to outsiders and suggested they sit on a bench outside the building.

When they were settled, Bach started her questioning. "First, I need to know your name, and your title. I assume that you are . . . what was it?" She consulted her notes, taken hastily from a display she had called up on the computer terminal in her office. "I don't seem to have found a title for you."

"We have none," the barbie said. "If you must think of a title, consider us as the keeper of records."

"All right. And your name?"

"We have no name."

Bach sighed. "Yes, I understand that you forsake names when you come here. But you had one before. You were given one at birth. I'm going to have to have it for my investigation."

The woman looked pained. "No, you don't understand. It is true that this body had a name at one time. But it has been wiped from this one's mind. It would cause this one a great deal of pain to be reminded of it." She stumbled verbally every time she said "this one." Evidently even a polite circumlocution of the personal pronoun was distressing.

"I'll try to get it from another angle, then." This was

already getting hard to deal with, Bach saw, and knew it could only get tougher. "You say you are the keeper of records."

"We are. We keep records because the law says we must. Each citizen must be recorded, or so we have been told."

"For a very good reason," Bach said. "We're going to need access to those records. For the investigation. You understand? I assume an officer has already been through them, or the deceased couldn't have been identified as Leah P. Ingraham."

"That's true. But it won't be necessary for you to go through the records again. We are here to confess. We murdered L. P. Ingraham, serial number 11005. We are surrendering peacefully. You may take us to your prison." She held out her hands, wrists close together, ready to be shackled.

Weil was startled, reached tentatively for his hand-cuffs, then looked to Bach for guidance.

"Let me get this straight. You're saying you're the one who did it? You, personally."

"That's correct. We did it. We have never defied temporal authority, and we are willing to pay the penalty."

"Once more." Bach reached out and grasped the barbie's wrist, forced the hand open, palm up. "*This* is the person, this is the body that committed the murder? This hand, this one right here, held the knife and killed Ingraham? This hand, as opposed to 'your' thousands of other hands?"

The barbie frowned.

"Put that way, no. *This* hand did not grasp the murder weapon. But *our* hand did. What's the difference?"

"Quite a bit, in the eyes of the law." Bach sighed, and let go of the woman's hand. Woman? She wondered if the term applied. She realized she needed to know more about Standardists. But it was convenient to think of them as such, since their faces were feminine.

"Let's try again. I'll need you—and the eyewitnesses to the crime—to study the tape of the murder. *I* can't tell the difference between the murderer, the victim, or any of the bystanders. But surely you must be able to. I assume that . . . well, like the old saying went, 'all Chinamen look alike.' That was to Caucasian races, of course. Orientals had no trouble telling each other apart. So I thought that you . . . that you people would . . ." She trailed off at the look of blank incomprehension on the barbie's face.

"We don't know what you're talking about."

Bach's shoulders slumped.

"You mean you can't . . . not even if you saw her again . . . ?"

The woman shrugged. "We all look the same to this one."

Anna-Louise Bach sprawled out on her flotation bed later that night, surrounded by scraps of paper. Untidy as it was, her thought processes were helped by actually scribbling facts on paper rather than filing them in her datalink. And she did her best work late at night, at home, in bed, after taking a bath or making love. Tonight she had done both and found she needed every bit of the invigorating clarity it gave her.

Standardists.

They were an offbeat religious sect founded ninety years earlier by someone whose name had not survived. That was not surprising, since Standardists gave up their names when they joined the order, made every effort consistent with the laws of the land to obliterate the name and person as if he or she had never existed. The epithet "barbie" had quickly been attached to them by the press. The origin of the word was a popular children's toy of the twentieth and early twenty-first centuries, a plastic, sexless, mass-produced "girl" doll with an elaborate wardrobe.

The barbies had done surprisingly well for a group which did not reproduce, which relied entirely on new members from the outside world to replenish their numbers. They had grown for twenty years, then reached a population stability where deaths equaled new members—which they call "components." They had suffered moderately from religious intolerance, moving from country to country until the majority had come to Luna sixty years ago.

They drew new components from the walking wounded of society, the people who had not done well in a world that preached conformity, passivity, and tolerance of your billions of neighbors, yet rewarded only those who were individualist and aggressive enough to stand apart from the herd. The barbies had opted out of a system where one had to be at once a face in the crowd and a proud individual with hopes and dreams and desires. They were the inheritors of a long tradition of ascetic withdrawal, surrendering their names, their bodies, and their temporal aspirations to a life that was ordered and easy to understand.

Bach realized she might be doing some of them a disservice in that evaluation. They were not necessarily all losers. There must be those among them who were attracted simply by the religious ideas of the sect, though Bach felt there was little in the teachings that made sense.

She skimmed through the dogma, taking notes. The Standardists preached the commonality of humanity, denigrated free will, and elevated the group and the consensus to demigod status. Nothing too unusual in the theory; it was the practice of it that made people queasy.

There was a creation theory and a godhead, who was not worshiped but contemplated. Creation happened when the Goddess—a prototypical earth-mother who had no name—gave birth to the universe. She put people in it, all alike, stamped from the same universal mold.

Sin entered the picture. One of the people began to wonder. This person had a name, given to him or her *after* the original sin as part of the punishment, but Bach could not find it written down anywhere. She decided that it was a dirty word which Standardists never told an outsider.

This person asked Goddess what it was all for. What had been wrong with the void, that Goddess had seen fit to fill it with people who didn't seem to have a reason for existing?

That was too much. For reasons unexplained—and impolite to even ask about—Goddess had punished humans by introducing differentness into the world. Warts, big noses, kinky hair, white skin, tall people and fat people and deformed people, blue eyes, body hair, freckles, testicles, and labia. A billion faces and fingerprints, each soul trapped in a body distinct from all others, with the heavy burden of trying to establish an identity in a perpetual shouting match.

But the faith held that peace was achieved in striving

to regain that lost Eden. When all humans were again the same person, Goddess would welcome them back. Life was a testing, a trial.

Bach certainly agreed with that. She gathered her notes and shuffled them together, then picked up the book she had brought back from Anytown. The barbie had given it to her when Bach asked for a picture of the murdered woman.

It was a blueprint for a human being.

The title was *The Book of Specifications. The Specs*, for short. Each barbie carried one, tied to her waist with a tape measure. It gave tolerances in engineering terms, defining what a barbie could look like. It was profusely illustrated with drawings of parts of the body in minute detail, giving measurements in millimeters.

She closed the book and sat up, propping her head on a pillow. She reached for her viewpad and propped it on her knees, punched the retrieval code for the murder tape. For the twentieth time that night, she watched a figure spring forward from a crowd of identical figures in the tube station, slash at Leah Ingraham, and melt back into the crowd as her victim lay bleeding and eviscerated on the floor.

She slowed it down, concentrating on the killer, trying to spot something different about her. Anything at all would do. The knife struck. Blood spurted. Barbies milled about in consternation. A few belatedly ran after the killer, not reacting fast enough. People seldom reacted quickly enough. But the killer had blood on her hand. Make a note to ask about that.

Bach viewed the film once more, saw nothing useful, and decided to call it a night.

The room was long and tall, brightly lit from strips high above. Bach followed the attendant down the rows of square locker doors that lined one wall. The air was cool and humid, the floor wet from a recent hosing.

The man consulted the card in his hand and pulled the metal handle on locker 659A, making a noise that echoed through the bare room. He slid the drawer out and lifted the sheet from the corpse.

It was not the first mutilated corpse Bach had seen, but it was the first nude barbie. She immediately noted the lack of nipples on the two hills of flesh that pretended to be breasts, and the smooth, unmarked skin in the crotch. The attendant was frowning, consulting the card on the corpse's foot.

"Some mistake here," he muttered. "Geez, the headaches. What do you do with a thing like that?" He scratched his head, then scribbled through the large letter "F" on the card, replacing it with a neat "N." He looked at Bach and grinned sheepishly. "What do you do?" he repeated.

Bach didn't much care what he did. She studied L. P. Ingraham's remains, hoping that something on the body would show her why a barbie had decided she must die.

There was little difficulty seeing *how* she had died. The knife had entered her abdomen, going deep, and the wound extended upward from there in a slash that ended beneath the breastbone. Part of the bone was cut through. The knife had been sharp, but it would have taken a powerful arm to slice through that much meat.

The attendant watched curiously as Bach pulled the dead woman's legs apart and studied what she saw there. She found the tiny slit of the urethra set back around the curve, just anterior to the anus.

Bach opened her copy of *The Specs*, took out a tape measure, and started to work.

"Mr. Atlas, I got your name from the Morphology Guide's files as a practitioner who's had a lot of dealings with the Standardist Church."

The man frowned, then shrugged. "So? You may not approve of them, but they're legal. And my records are in order. I don't do any work on anybody until the police have checked for a criminal record." He sat on the edge of the desk in the spacious consulting room, facing Bach. Mr. Rock Atlas—surely a *nom de métier*—had shoulders carved from granite, teeth like flashing pearls, and the face of a young god. He was a walking, flexing advertisement for his profession. Bach crossed her legs nervously. She had always had a taste for beef.

"I'm not investigating you, Mr. Atlas. This is a murder case, and I'd appreciate your cooperation."

"Call me Rock," he said, with a winning smile.

"Must I? Very well. I came to ask you what you would do, how long the work would take, if I asked to be converted to a barbie."

His face fell. "Oh, no, what a tragedy! I can't allow it. My dear, it would be a crime." He reached over to her and touched her chin lightly, turning her head. "No, Lieutenant, for you I'd build up the hollows in the cheeks just the slightest bit—maybe tighten up the muscles behind them—then drift the orbital bones out a little bit farther from the nose to set your eyes wider. More attention-getting, you understand. That touch of mystery. Then of course, there's your nose."

She pushed his hand away and shook her head. "No, I'm not coming to you for the operation. I just want to know. How much work would it entail, and how close can you come to the specs of the church?" Then she frowned and looked at him suspiciously. "What's wrong with my nose?"

"Well, my dear, I didn't mean to imply there was anything *wrong*; in fact, it has a certain overbearing power that must be useful to you once in a while, in the circles you move in. Even the lean to the left could be justified, aesthetically—"

"Never mind," she said, angry at herself for having fallen into his sales pitch. "Just answer my question."

He studied her carefully, asked her to stand up and turn around. She was about to object that she had not necessarily meant herself personally as the surgical candidate, just a woman in general, when he seemed to lose interest in her.

"It wouldn't be much of a job," he said. "Your height is just slightly over the parameters; I could take that out of your thighs and lower legs, maybe shave some vertebrae. Take out some fat here and put it back there. Take off those nipples and dig out your uterus and ovaries, sew up your crotch. With a man, chop off the penis. I'd have to break up your skull a little and shift the bones around, then build up the face from there. Say two days work, one overnight and one outpatient."

"And when you were through, what would be left to identify me?"

"Say that again?"

Bach briefly explained her situation, and Atlas pondered it.

"You've got a problem. I take off the fingerprints and footprints. I don't leave any external scars, not even microscopic ones. No moles, freckles, warts, or birthmarks; they all have to go. A blood test would work, and so would a retinal print. An X ray of the skull. A voiceprint would be questionable. I even that out as much as possible. I can't think of anything else."

"Nothing that could be seen from a purely visual exam?"

"That's the whole point of the operation, isn't it?"

"I know. I was just hoping you might know something even the barbies were not aware of. Thank you, anyway."

He got up, took her hand, and kissed it. "No trouble. And if you ever decide to get that nose taken care of . . ."

She met Jorge Weil at the temple gate in the middle of Anytown. He had spent his morning there, going through the records, and she could see the work didn't agree with him. He took her back to the small office where the records were kept in battered file cabinets. There was a barbie waiting for them there. She spoke without preamble.

"We decided at equalization last night to help you as much as possible."

"Oh, yeah? Thanks. I wondered if you would, considering what happened fifty years ago."

Weil looked puzzled. "What was that?"

Bach waited for the barbie to speak, but she evidently wasn't going to.

"All right. I found it last night. The Standardists were involved in murder once before, not long after they came to Luna. You notice you never see one of them in New Dresden?"

Weil shrugged. "So what? They keep to themselves."

"They were *ordered* to keep to themselves. At first, they could move freely like any other citizens. Then one of them killed somebody—not a Standardist this time. It was known the murderer was a barbie; there were witnesses. The police started looking for the killer. You guess what happened."

"They ran into the problems we're having." Weil grimaced. "It doesn't look so good, does it?"

"It's hard to be optimistic," Bach conceded. "The

killer was never found. The barbies offered to surrender one of their number at random, thinking the law would be satisfied with that. But of course, it wouldn't do. There was a public outcry, and a lot of pressure to force them to adopt some kind of distinguishing characteristic, like a number tattooed on their foreheads. I don't think that would have worked, either. It could have been covered.

"The fact is that the barbies were seen as a menace to society. They could kill at will and blend back into their community like grains of sand on a beach. We would be powerless to punish a guilty party. There was no provision in the law for dealing with them."

Bach sighed. "I want to see the witnesses to the crime. I might as well start interviewing them."

In short order, thirteen barbies were brought. Bach intended to question them thoroughly to see if their stories were consistent, and if they had changed.

She sat them down and took them one at a time, and almost immediately ran into a stone wall. It took her several minutes to see the problem, frustrating minutes spent trying to establish which of the barbies had spoken to the officer first, which second, and so forth.

"Hold it. Listen carefully. Was this body physically present at the time of the crime? Did these eyes see it happen?"

The barbie's brow furrowed. "Why, no. But does it matter?"

"It does to me, babe. *Hey, twenty-three thousand!*"

The barbie stuck her head in the door. Bach looked pained.

"I need the actual people who were *there*. Not thirteen picked at random."

"The story is known to all."

Bach spent five minutes explaining that it made a difference to her, then waited an hour as 23900 located the people who were actual witnesses.

And again she hit a stone wall. The stories were absolutely identical, which she knew to be impossible. Observers *always* report events differently. They make themselves the hero, invent things before and after they first began observing, rearrange and edit and interpret. But not the barbies. Bach struggled for an hour, trying to shake one of them, and got nowhere. She was facing a consensus, something that had been discussed among the barbies until an account of the event had emerged and then been accepted as truth. It was probably a close approximation, but it did Bach no good. She needed discrepancies to gnaw at, and there were none.

Worst of all, she was convinced no one was lying to her. Had she questioned the thirteen random choices, she would have gotten the same answers. They would have thought of themselves as having been there, since some of them had been and they had been told about it. What happened to one, happened to all.

Her options were evaporating fast. She dismissed the witnesses, called 23900 back in, and sat her down. Bach ticked off points on her fingers.

"One. Do you have the personal effects of the deceased?"

"We have no private property."

Bach nodded. "Two. Can you take me to her room?"

"We each sleep in any room we find available at night. There is no—"

"Right. Three. Any friends or coworkers I might . . ." Bach rubbed her forehead with one hand. "Right. Skip it. Four. What was her job? Where did she work?"

"All jobs are interchangeable here. We work at what needs—"

"*Right!*" Bach exploded. She got up and paced the floor. "What the hell do you expect me to *do* with a situation like this? I don't have *anything* to work with, not one snuffin' *thing*. No way of telling *why* she was killed, no way to pick out the *killer*, no way . . . ah, *shit*. What do you expect me to *do?*"

"We don't expect you to do anything," the barbie said, quietly. "We didn't ask you to come here. We'd like it very much if you just went away."

In her anger Bach had forgotten that. She was stopped, unable to move in any direction. Finally she caught Weil's eye and jerked her head toward the door.

"Let's get out of here." Weil said nothing. He followed Bach out the door and hurried to catch up.

They reached the tube station, and Bach stopped out-side their waiting capsule. She sat down heavily on a bench, put her chin on her palm, and watched the antlike mass of barbies working at the loading dock.

"Any ideas?"

Weil shook his head, sitting beside her and removing his cap to wipe sweat from his forehead.

"They keep it too hot in here," he said. Bach nodded, not really hearing him. She watched the group of barbies as two separated themselves from the crowd and came a few steps in her direction. Both were laughing, as if at some private joke, looking right at Bach. One of them reached under her blouse and withdrew a long, gleaming steel knife. In one smooth motion she plunged it into the other barbie's stomach and lifted, bringing her up on the balls of her feet. The one who had been stabbed looked surprised for a moment, staring down at herself, her mouth open as the knife gutted her like a fish. Then her eyes widened and she stared horror-stricken at her companion, and slowly went to her knees, holding the knife to her as blood gushed out and soaked her white uniform.

"*Stop her!*" Bach shouted. She was on her feet and running, after a moment of horrified paralysis. It had looked *so* much like the tape.

She was about forty meters from the killer, who moved with deliberate speed, jogging rather than running. She passed the barbie who had been attacked—and who was now on her side, still holding the knife hilt almost tenderly to herself, wrapping her body around the pain. Bach thumbed the panic button on her communicator, glanced over her shoulder to see Weil kneeling beside the stricken barbie, then looked back—

—to a confusion of running figures. Which one was it? *Which one?*

She grabbed the one who seemed to be in the same place and moving in the same direction as the killer had been before she looked away. She swung the barbie around and hit her hard on the side of the neck with the edge of her palm, watched her fall while trying to look at all the other barbies at the same time. They were running in both directions, some trying to get away, others entering the loading dock to see what was going on. It was a madhouse scene with shrieks and shouts and baffling movement.

Bach spotted something bloody lying on the floor, then knelt by the inert figure and clapped the handcuffs on her. She looked up into a sea of faces, all alike.

The commissioner dimmed the lights, and he, Bach, and Weil faced the big screen at the end of the room. Beside the screen was a department photoanalyst with a pointer in her hand. The tape began to run.

"Here they are," the woman said, indicating two barbies with the tip of the long stick. They were just faces on the edge of the crowd, beginning to move. "Victim right here, the suspect to her right." Everyone watched as the stabbing was re-created. Bach winced when she saw how long she had taken to react. In her favor, it had taken Weil a fraction of a second longer.

"Lieutenant Bach begins to move here. The suspect moves back toward the crowd. If you'll notice, she is watching Bach over her shoulder. Now. Here." She froze a frame. "Bach loses eye contact. The suspect peels off the plastic glove which prevented blood from staining her hand. She drops it, moves laterally. By the time Back looks back, we can see she is after the wrong suspect."

Bach watched in sick fascination as her image assaulted the wrong barbie, the actual killer only a meter to her left. The tape resumed normal speed, and Bach watched the killer until her eyes began to hurt from not blinking. She would not lose her this time.

"She's incredibly brazen. She does not leave the room for another twenty minutes." Bach saw herself kneel and help the medical team load the wounded barbie into the capsule. The killer had been at her elbow, almost touching her. She felt her arm break out in goose pimples.

She remembered the sick fear that had come over her as she knelt by the injured woman. *It could be any of them. The one behind me, for instance . . .*

She had drawn her weapon then, backed against the wall, and not moved until the reinforcements arrived a few minutes later.

At a motion from the commissioner, the lights came back on.

"Let's hear what you have," he said.

Bach glanced at Weil, then read from her notebook.

" 'Sergeant Weil was able to communicate with the victim shortly before medical help arrived. He asked her if she knew anything pertinent as to the identity of her assailant. She answered no, saying only that it was "the wrath." She could not elaborate.' I quote now from the account Sergeant Weil wrote down immediately after the interview. ' "It hurts, it hurts." "I'm dying, I'm dying." I told her help was on the way. She responded: "I'm dying." Victim became incoherent, and I attempted to get a shirt from the onlookers to stop the flow of blood. No cooperation was forthcoming.' "

"It was the word 'I,' " Weil supplied. "When she said that, they all started to drift away."

" 'She became rational once more,' " Bach resumed, " 'long enough to whisper a number to me. The number was twelve-fifteen, which I wrote down as one-two-one-five. She roused herself once more, said, "I'm dying." ' " Bach closed the notebook and looked up. "Of course, she was right." She coughed nervously.

"We invoked section 35b of the New Dresden Unified Code, 'Hot Pursuit,' suspending civil liberties locally for the duration of the search. We located component 1215 by the simple expedient of lining up all the barbies and having them pull their pants down. Each has a serial number in the small of her back. Component 1215, one Sylvester J. Cronhausen, is in custody at this moment.

"While the search was going on, we went to sleeping cubicle 1215 with a team of criminologists. In a concealed compartment beneath the bunk we found these items." Bach got up, opened the evidence bag, and spread the items on the table.

There was a carved wooden mask. It had a huge nose with a hooked end, a mustache, and a fringe of black hair around it. Beside the mask were several jars of powders and creams, greasepaint, and cologne. One black nylon sweater, one pair black trousers, one pair black sneakers. A stack of pictures clipped from magazines, showing ordinary people, many of them wearing more clothes than was normal in Luna. There was a black wig and a merkin of the same color.

"What was that last?" the commissioner asked.

"A merkin, sir," Bach supplied. "A pubic wig."

"Ah." He contemplated the assortment, leaned back in his chair. "Somebody liked to dress up."

"Evidently, sir." Bach stood at ease with her hands clasped behind her back, her face passive. She felt an acute sense of failure, and a cold determination to get the woman with the gall to stand at her elbow after committing murder before her eyes. She was sure the time and place had been chosen deliberately, that the barbie had been executed for Bach's benefit.

"Do you think these items belonged to the deceased?"

"We have no reason to state that, sir," Bach said. "However, the circumstances are suggestive."

"Of what?"

"I can't be sure. These things *might* have belonged to the victim. A random search of other cubicles turned up nothing like this. We showed the items to component 23900, our liaison. She professed not to know their purpose." She stopped, then added, "I believe she was lying. She looked quite disgusted."

"Did you arrest her?"

"No, sir. I didn't think it wise. She's the only connection we have, such as she is."

The commissioner frowned, and laced his fingers together. "I'll leave it up to you, Lieutenant Bach. Frankly, we'd like to be shut of this mess as soon as possible."

"I couldn't agree with you more, sir."

"Perhaps you don't understand me. We have to have a warm body to indict. We have to have one soon."

"Sir, I'm doing the best I can. Candidly, I'm beginning to wonder if there's anything I *can* do."

"You still don't understand me." He looked around the office. The stenographer and photoanalyst had left. He was alone with Bach and Weil. He flipped a switch on his desk, turning a recorder *off*, Bach realized.

"The news is picking up on this story. We're beginning to get some heat. On the one hand, people are afraid of these barbies. They're hearing about the murder fifty years ago, and the informal agreement. They don't like it much. On the other hand, there's the civil libertarians. They'll fight hard to prevent anything happening to the barbies, on principle. The government doesn't want to get into a mess like that. I can hardly blame them.''

Bach said nothing, and the commissioner looked pained.

"I see I have to spell it out. We have a suspect in custody," he said.

"Are you referring to component 1215, Sylvester Cronhausen?"

"No. I'm speaking of the one you captured."

"Sir, the tape clearly shows she is not the guilty party. She was an innocent bystander." She felt her face heat up as she said it. Damn it; she had tried her best.

"Take a look at this." He pressed a button and the tape began to play again. But the quality was much impaired. There were bursts of snow, moments when the picture faded out entirely. It was a very good imitation of a camera failing. Bach watched herself running through the crowd—there was a flash of white—and she had hit the woman. The lights came back on in the room.

"I've checked with the analyst. She'll go along. There's a bonus in this, for both of you." He looked from Weil to Bach.

"I don't think I can go through with that, sir."

He looked like he'd tasted a lemon. "I didn't say we were doing this today. It's an option. But I ask you to look at it this way, just look at it, and I'll say no more. This is the way *they themselves* want it. They offered you the same deal the first time you were there. Close the case with a confession, no mess. We've already got this prisoner. She just says she killed her, she killed all of them. I want you to ask yourself, is she wrong? By her own lights and moral values? She believes she shares responsibility for the murders, and society demands a culprit. What's wrong with accepting their compromise and letting this all blow over?"

"Sir, it doesn't feel right to me. This is not in the oath I took. I'm supposed to protect the innocent, and she's innocent. She's the *only* barbie I *know* to be innocent."

The commissioner sighed. "Bach, you've got four days. You give me an alternative by then."

"Yes, sir. If I can't, I'll tell you now that I won't inter-

fere with what you plan. But you'll have to accept my resigna-
tion."

Anna-Louise Bach reclined in the bathtub with her head pil-
lowed on a folded towel. Only her neck, nipples, and knees
stuck out above the placid surface of the water, tinted purple
with a generous helping of bath salts. She clenched a thin
cheroot in her teeth. A ribbon of lavender smoke curled from
the end of it, rising to join the cloud near the ceiling.

She reached up with one foot and turned on the taps,
letting out cooled water and refilling with hot until the sweat
broke out on her brow. She had been in the tub for several
hours. The tips of her fingers were like washboards.

There seemed to be few alternatives. The barbies were
foreign to her, and to anyone she could assign to interview
them. They didn't want her help in solving the crimes. All
the old rules and procedures were useless. Witnesses meant
nothing; one could not tell one from the next, nor separate
their stories. Opportunity? Several thousand individuals had
it. Motive was a blank. She had a physical description in
minute detail, even tapes of the actual murders. Both were
useless.

There was one course of action that might show results.
She had been soaking for hours in the hope of determining
just how important her job was to her.

Hell, what else did she want to do?

She got out of the tub quickly, bringing a lot of water
with her to drip onto the floor. She hurried into her bedroom,
pulled the sheets off the bed, and slapped the nude male figure
on the buttocks.

"Come on, Svengali," she said. "Here's your chance
to do something about my nose."

She used every minute while her eyes were functioning to read
all she could find about Standardists. When Atlas worked on
her eyes, the computer droned into an earphone. She memorized most of the *Book of Standards*.

Ten hours of surgery, followed by eight hours flat on

her back, paralyzed, her body undergoing forced regeneration, her eyes scanning the words that flew by on an overhead screen.

Three hours of practice, getting used to shorter legs and arms. Another hour to assemble her equipment.

When she left the Atlas clinic, she felt she would pass for a barbie as long as she kept her clothes on. She hadn't gone *that* far.

People tended to forget about access locks that led to the surface. Bach had used the fact more than once to show up in places where no one expected her.

She parked her rented crawler by the lock and left it there. Moving awkwardly in her pressure suit, she entered and started it cycling, then stepped through the inner door into an equipment room in Anytown. She stowed the suit, checked herself quickly in a washroom mirror, straightened the tape measure that belted her loose white jumpsuit, and entered the darkened corridors.

What she was doing was not illegal in any sense, but she was on edge. She didn't expect the barbies to take kindly to her masquerade if they discovered it, and she knew how easy it was for a barbie to vanish forever. Three had done so before Bach ever got the case.

The place seemed deserted. It was late evening by the arbitrary day cycle of New Dresden. Time for the nightly equalization. Bach hurried down the silent hallways to the main meeting room in the temple.

It was full of barbies and a vast roar of conversation. Bach had no trouble slipping in, and in a few minutes she knew her facial work was as good as Atlas had promised.

Equalization was the barbies' way of standardizing experience. They had been unable to simplify their lives to the point where each member of the community experienced the same things every day; the *Book of Standards* said it was a goal to be aimed for, but probably unattainable this side of Holy Reassimilation with Goddess. They tried to keep the available jobs easy enough that each member could do them all. The commune did not seek to make a profit; but air, water, and food had to be purchased, along with replacement parts and services to keep things running. The community had to produce things to trade with the outside.

They sold luxury items: hand-carved religious statues, illuminated holy books, painted crockery, and embroidered tapestries. None of the items were Standardist. The barbies had no religious symbols except their uniformity and the tape measure, but nothing in their dogma prevented them from selling objects of reverence to people of other faiths.

Bach had seen the products for sale in the better shops. They were meticulously produced, but suffered from the fact that each item looked too much like every other. People buying hand-produced luxuries in a technological age tend to want the differences that nonmachine production entails, whereas the barbies wanted everything to look exactly alike. It was an ironic situation, but the barbies willingly sacrificed value by adhering to their standards.

Each barbie did things during the day that were as close as possible to what everyone else had done. But someone had to cook meals, tend the air machines, load the freight. Each component had a different job each day. At equalization, they got together and tried to even that out.

It was boring. Everyone talked at once, to anyone who happened to be around. Each woman told what she had done that day. Bach heard the same group of stories a hundred times before the night was over, and repeated them to anyone who would listen.

Anything unusual was related over a loudspeaker so everyone could be aware of it and thus spread out the intolerable burden of anomaly. No barbie wanted to keep a unique experience to herself; it made her soiled, unclean, until it was shared by all.

Bach was getting very tired of it—she was short on sleep—when the lights went out. The buzz of conversation shut off as if a tape had broken.

"All cats are alike in the dark," someone muttered, quite near Bach. Then a single voice was raised. It was solemn; almost a chant.

"We are the wrath. There is blood on our hands, but it is the holy blood of cleansing. We have told you of the cancer eating at the heart of the body, and yet still you cower away from what must be done. *The filth must be removed from us!*"

Bach was trying to tell which direction the words were coming from in the total darkness. Then she became aware of movement, people brushing against her, all going in the same direction. She began to buck the tide when she realized everyone was moving away from the voice.

"You think you can use our holy uniformity to hide among us, but the vengeful hand of Goddess will not be stayed. The mark is upon you, our onetime sisters. Your sins have set you apart and retribution will strike swiftly.

"*There are five of you left.* Goddess knows who you are, and will not tolerate your perversion of her holy truth. Death will strike you when you least expect it. Goddess sees the differentness within you, the differentness you seek but hope to hide from your upright sisters."

People were moving more swiftly now, and a scuffle had developed ahead of her. She struggled free of people who were breathing panic from every pore, until she stood in a clear space. The speaker was shouting to be heard over the sound of whimpering and the shuffling of bare feet. Bach moved forward, swinging her outstretched hands. But another hand brushed her first.

The punch was not centered on her stomach, but it drove the air from her lungs and sent her sprawling. Someone tripped over her, and she realized things would get pretty bad if she didn't get to her feet. She was struggling up when the lights came back on.

There was a mass sigh of relief as each barbie examined her neighbor. Bach half expected another body to be found, but that didn't seem to be the case. The killer had vanished again.

She slipped away from the equalization before it began to break up, and hurried down the deserted corridors to room 1215.

She sat in the room—little more than a cell, with a bunk, a chair, and a light on a table—for more than two hours before the door opened, as she had hoped it would. A barbie stepped inside, breathing hard, closed the door, and leaned against it.

"We wondered if you would come," Bach said, tentatively.

The woman ran to Bach and collapsed at her knees, sobbing.

"Forgive us, please forgive us, our darling. We didn't dare come last night. We were afraid that . . . that if . . . that it might have been you who was murdered, and that the wrath would be waiting for us here. Forgive us, forgive us."

"It's all right," Bach said, for lack of anything better. Suddenly the barbie was on top of her, kissing her with a desperate passion. Bach was startled, though she had expected something of the sort. She responded as best she could. The barbie finally began to talk again.

"We must stop this, we just have to stop. We're so frightened of the wrath, but . . . but the *longing*! We can't stop ourselves. We need to see you so badly that we can hardly get through the day, not knowing if you are across town or working at our elbow. It builds all day, and at night, we cannot stop ourselves from sinning yet again." She was crying, more softly this time, not from happiness at seeing the woman she took Bach to be, but from a depth of desperation. "What's going to become of us?" she asked, helplessly.

"Shhh," Bach soothed. "It's going to be all right."

She comforted the barbie for a while, then saw her lift her head. Her eyes seemed to glow with a strange light.

"I can't wait any longer," she said. She stood up, and began taking off her clothes. Bach could see her hands shaking.

Beneath her clothing the barbie had concealed a few things that looked familiar. Bach could see that the merkin was already in place between her legs. There was a wooden mask much like the one that had been found in the secret panel, and a jar. The barbie unscrewed the top of it and used her middle finger to smear dabs of brown onto her breasts, making stylized nipples.

"Look what *I* got," she said, coming down hard on the pronoun her voice trembling. She pulled a flimsy yellow blouse from the pile of clothing on the floor, and slipped it over her shoulders. She struck a pose, then strutted up and down the tiny room.

"Come on, darling," she said. "Tell me how beautiful I am. Tell me I'm lovely. Tell me I'm the only one for you.

The only one. What's the *matter*? Are you still frightened? I'm not. I'll dare anything for you, my one and only love." But now she stopped walking and looked suspiciously at Bach. "Why aren't you getting dressed?"

"We . . . uh, I can't," Bach said, extemporizing. "They, uh, someone found the things. They're all gone." She didn't dare remove her clothes, because her nipples and pubic hair would look too real, even in the dim light.

The barbie was backing away. She picked up her mask and held it protectively to her. "What do you mean? Was she here? The wrath? Are they after us? It's true, isn't it? They can see us." She was on the edge of crying again, near panic.

"No, no, I think it was the police—" But it was doing no good. The barbie was at the door now, and had it half-open.

"You're her! What have you done to . . . No, no, you stay away." She reached into the clothing that she now held in her hand, and Bach hesitated for a moment, expecting a knife. It was enough time for the barbie to dart quickly through the door, slamming it behind her.

When Bach reached the door, the woman was gone.

Bach kept reminding herself that she was not here to find the other potential victims—of whom her visitor was certainly one—but to catch the killer. The fact remained that she wished she could have detained her, to question her further.

The woman was a pervert, by the only definition that made any sense among the Standardists. She, and presumably the other dead barbies, had an individuality fetish. When Bach had realized that, her first thought had been to wonder why they didn't simply leave the colony and become whatever they wished. But then why did a Christian seek out prostitutes? For the taste of sin. In the larger world, what these barbies did would have had little meaning. Here, it was sin of the worst and tastiest kind.

And somebody didn't like it at all.

The door opened again, and the woman stood there facing Bach, her hair disheveled, breathing hard.

"We had to come back," she said. "We're so sorry that we panicked like that. Can you forgive us?" She was coming toward Bach now, her arms out. She looked so vulnerable and contrite that Bach was astonished when the fist connected with her cheek.

Bach thudded against the wall, then found herself pinned under the woman's knees, with something sharp and cool against her throat. She swallowed very carefully, and said nothing. Her throat itched unbearably.

"She's dead," the barbie said. "And you're next." But there was something in her face that Bach didn't understand. The barbie brushed at her eyes a few times, and squinted down at her.

"Listen, I'm not who you think I am. If you kill me, you'll be bringing more trouble on your sisters than you can imagine."

The barbie hesitated, then roughly thrust her hand down into Bach's pants. Her eyes widened when she felt the genitals, but the knife didn't move. Bach knew she had to talk fast, and say all the right things.

"You understand what I'm talking about, don't you?" She looked for a response, but saw none. "You're aware of the political pressures that are coming down. You know this whole colony could be wiped out if you look like a threat to the outside. You don't want that."

"If it must be, it will be," the barbie said. "The purity is the important thing. If we die, we shall die pure. The blasphemers must be killed."

"I don't care about that anymore," Bach said, and finally got a ripple of interest from the barbie. "I have my principles, too. Maybe I'm not as fanatical about them as you are about yours. But they're important to me. One is that the guilty be brought to justice."

"You have the guilty party. Try her. Execute her. She will not protest."

"*You* are the guilty party."

The woman smiled. "So arrest us."

"All right, all right. I can't, obviously. Even if you don't kill me, you'll walk out that door and I'll never be able to find you. I've given up on that. I just don't have the time. This was my last chance, and it looks like it didn't work."

"We didn't think you could do it, even with more time. But why should we let you live?"

"Because we can help each other." She felt the pressure ease up a little, and managed to swallow again. "You don't want to kill me, because it could destroy your community. Myself . . . I need to be able to salvage some self-respect out of this mess. I'm willing to accept your definition of morality and let you be the law in your own community. Maybe you're even right. Maybe you *are* one being. But I can't let that woman be convicted, when I *know* she didn't kill anyone."

The knife was not touching her neck now, but it was still being held so that the barbie could plunge it into her throat at the slightest movement.

"And if we let you live? What do you get out of it? How do you free your 'innocent' prisoner?"

"Tell me where to find the body of the woman you just killed. I'll take care of the rest."

The pathology team had gone and Anytown was settling down once again. Bach sat on the edge of the bed with Jorge Weil. She was as tired as she ever remembered being. How long had it been since she slept?

"I'll tell you," Weil said, "I honestly didn't think this thing would work. I guess I was wrong."

Bach sighed. "I wanted to take her alive, Jorge. I thought I could. But when she came at me with the knife . . ." She let him finish the thought, not caring to lie to him. She'd already done that to the interviewer. In her story, she had taken the knife from her assailant and tried to disable her, but was forced in the end to kill her. Luckily, she had the bump on the back of her head from being thrown against the wall. It made a blackout period plausible. Otherwise, someone would have wondered why she waited so long to call for police and an ambulance. The barbie had been dead for an hour when they arrived.

"Well, I'll hand it to you. You sure pulled this out. I'll admit it, I was having a hard time deciding if I'd do as you were going to do and resign, or if I could have stayed on. Now I'll never know."

"Maybe it's best that way. I don't really know, either."

Jorge grinned at her. "I can't get used to thinking of *you* being behind that god-awful face."

"Neither can I, and I don't want to see any mirrors. I'm going straight to Atlas and get it changed back." She got wearily to her feet and walked toward the tube station with Weil.

She had not quite told him the truth. She did intend to get her own face back as soon as possible—nose and all—but there was one thing left to do.

From the first, a problem that had bothered her had been the question of how the killer identified her victims.

Presumably the perverts had arranged times and places to meet for their strange rites. That would have been easy enough. Any one barbie could easily shirk her duties. She could say she was sick, and no one would know it was the same barbie who had been sick yesterday, and for a week or month before. She need not work; she could wander the halls acting as if she were on her way from one job to another. No one could challenge her. Likewise, while 23900 had said no barbie spent consecutive nights in the same room, there was no way for her to know that. Evidently room 1215 had been taken over permanently by the perverts.

And the perverts would have no scruples about identifying each other by serial number at their clandestine meetings, though they could do it in the streets. The killer didn't even have that.

But someone had known how to identify them, to pick them out of a crowd. Bach thought she must have infiltrated meetings, marked the participants in some way. One could lead her to another, until she knew them all and was ready to strike.

She kept recalling the strange way the killer had looked at her, the way she had squinted. The mere fact that she had not killed Bach instantly in a case of mistaken identity meant she had been expecting to see something that had not been there.

And she had an idea about that.

She meant to go to the morgue first, and to examine the corpses under different wavelengths of lights, with various filters. She was betting some kind of mark would become visible on the faces, a mark the killer had been looking for with her contact lenses.

It had to be something that was visible only with the

right kind of equipment, or under the right circumstances. If she kept at it long enough, she would find it.

If it was an invisible ink, it brought up another interesting question. How had it been applied? With a brush or spray gun? Unlikely. But such an ink on the killer's hands might look and feel like water.

Once she had marked her victims, the killer would have to be confident the mark would stay in place for a reasonable time. The murders had stretched over a month. So she was looking for an indelible, invisible ink, one that soaked into pores.

And if it was indelible . . .

There was no use thinking further about it. She was right, or she was wrong. When she struck the bargain with the killer she had faced up to the possibility that she might have to live with it. Certainly she could not now bring a killer into court, not after what she had just said.

No, if she came back to Anytown and found a barbie whose hands were stained with guilt, she would have to do the job herself.

BARBIE'S LITTLE SISTER

Ellie Schoenfeld

Barbie's little sister
Aurora
got sent away to reform school
when she was thirteen.
Mattel brought her back complete
with wheat germ, a VW love bus
and a recipe for sesame dream bars.
But she never caught on.
Didn't go for the vanity
table or the bubble head.
Thought Barbie was repressed
and Ken was a nerd
so she hit the road
with his cousin Jeremy.
They went to demonstrations
wore love beads
and got matching tattoos.
Finally Mattel stopped marketing her,
didn't think she'd make
a good role model.

BARBIE DISAPPEARED ONE DAY

Ellie Schoenfeld

There was lots of speculation,
kidnap, foul play
maybe a Jimmy Hoffa kind of thing.
The National Enquirer once linked them
together in the exposé
"Where Dolls and Mobsters Meet."
Actually she just got sick
of the fame thing
and joined her real-life lover
Elvis
who had been hiding out in Michigan
but had to move
once the tabloids found him.
Moved to Chicago
which is where Barbie found him
working as a roadie
for some of the local bands
and shooting up everything
he could melt down.
Eventually the needle found its way
to Barbie and the little-known vein
that ran up her plastic arm.
And that's how they lived and loved
on the lower east side
closer to Jimmy than they thought
until finally they got busted

in a small-time liquor store holdup.
Elvis escaped, busted out
in a gust of wind
aided by his old sky-god buddy.
Barbie got sent downtown
where she confounded the authorities
by having no fingerprints,
aggravated the telephone operator
by insisting
that Midge and Skipper
didn't have any last names.

BARBIE: A MEMOIR

Sparrow

I spent only one year as a junkie, and it was a year I didn't need anyway. I had just graduated college, in art history, and worked in a taco shop in Ithaca, New York. In retrospect, it was a productive year. I wrote my first novel (a fictional biography of Antoine-Joseph Sax, inventor of the saxophone), lobbied for the impeachment of Ronald Reagan, learned chess, and studied Islam in a small mosque at the edge of town.

It was then that I met Barbie. She must have been twenty-five. She was a speed freak. She frequented the same bar I did—a melancholy dive with a nautical motif, called The Sloop.

Barbie was obviously an addict—her eyes had that hollow, shapeless look. She was a *quiet* speed freak, too. When you know hundreds of meth heads, you'll meet three or four quiet ones.

Barbie had remarkable perception. She could notice an eccentric key chain at fifty feet, or overhear two conversations at once, with complete accuracy.

I'd always found her attractive. My sister had had one of her dolls, as a child. That attenuated, *airline* look—Barbie resembled a stewardess *and* an airplane—was always, for me, the purest American beauty. As an addict, Barbie's charm increased; her face had the luminosity of a lampshade.

I slept with her once, simply because she had stayed till three at my house, and saw no point in leaving. In bed, she was earnest, yet reserved. The word that comes to mind is *tact*; she was a tactful lover.

She and I would play chess for hours. She won 90 percent of the time, though I was studying with a Master.

"I just took Barbie's rook!" I'd think to myself with amazement.

She only spoke of Ken once. "He was a shit," she said, while drunk. I had a suspicion he was somehow behind her dissipation.

I put her on a bus to Seattle in 1986, knowing I would never see her again. That day she was suddenly voluble. "I threw out all my Talking Heads records!" she said, with an enormous smile. "Maybe I'll go back to school and become a chiropractor!"

I'm sure she never became a chiropractor.

NAVY BARBIE

Lyn Lifshin

wants to see the world,
she does get a little
seasick but likes
the white uniform, tho
the skirt is a little
too loose and long for
her taste. Still it might
be a change she can go
with. Actually the sequins
dug into her shoulders,
the ballerina tulle
scratched, and tho it was
kept secret, fun fur
made her sneeze. And
forget the Parisian
Bonjour look: that was
the worst, a cameo
choker size of a plum
or a small coconut
wedged against her larynx,
so she says when I try
to say yes or no it
scraped, and the lace
under my arms—talk
about sandpaper. But
the worst was those fish
net hose, rough, and the
garter, Jesus, grating,

my toes burned from that
pattern, crammed into
high-heeled platform
open-toes and the hair
piece with feathers. At
least in the navy they've
actually, she smiles,
given me something to
read. My hair is natural.
I'm authentic. First
Class Petty Officer.
I finally am more than
just a pretty: I rank

BARBIE HUNTS THRU MEDICAL BOOKS LOOKING FOR WHAT IS WRONG WITH HER WHEN SHE SEES HER BIRTH DATE IN A BOOK, KNOWS SHE IS OVER 30

Lyn Lifshin

and feels so
hollow inside,
unfulfilled,
as if all she's
done is change
her clothes.
She wonders
about the women's
movement, maybe,
she frowns, it's
the change and
she hasn't even
had a baby, had
a period, a
hair that was
not in place.
Perfection that
can be shelved,
one yank, she
shivers, and I'd

be bald, naked.
She flips thru
chapters on
neurosis, wonders
if it's hormones
she lacks. Where
she's been hardly
seems to matter:
the beach, Sun
Valley, Spain.
It's all facade,
going thru the
motions. What
did a wedding
get me, she groans,
I never was free-
moving, as they
said in 1975,
but empty, full
of holes—some
thing just for
someone else
to collect
or abuse

BARBIE WONDERS ABOUT BUYING A COFFIN

Lyn Lifshin

if she'll need one,
not that these
plastic boxes she's
in so long on a
shelf aren't like
being buried in a
toy box under eaves,
freezing in winter,
scorched by June.
She wonders if they
will bury her in a
ballerina costume,
a rodeo suit, if
they'll shave her
hair or braid it.
Just because she's
empty, she frowns,
doesn't mean she
doesn't care. Or
that her velvet or
tulle, even her
underpants have
been stripped from
her and she's been
left nude as some
one in the camps

about to march into
gas doesn't mean
she doesn't want
to know if she'll
go with one of her
many scarves around
her, a la Isadora,
or if Ken, supposing
she's eyeing a Ricky
or P.T. or Alan,
Skipper or maybe
even trying Christy,
rages in, beans her
with his boogie board,
strangles her with
the ropes of his
Hawaian fun hammock
or stuffs her to
suffocation with
fruit snacks and palm
leaves or poisons her
with cyanide in soda
from the All-American
Store, runs her over
in a remote-control
Corvette with head-
lights that glow and
leaves her in the trunk
with nothing to wear
for this last stop

FLOOR SHOW

Julia Alvarez

*N*o elbows, no Cokes, only milk or—" Mami paused. Which of her four girls could fill in the blank of how they were to behave at the restaurant with the Fannings?

"No elbows on the table," Sandi guessed.

"She already said that," Carla accused.

"No fighting, girls!" Mami scolded them all and continued The Epistle. "Only milk or ice water. And I make your orders. Is that clear?"

The four braided and beribboned heads nodded. At moments like this when they all seemed one organism—*the four girls*—Sandi would get that yearning to wander off into the United States of America by herself and never come back as the second of four girls so close in age.

This time, though, she nodded. Mami's tone of voice did not invite contradiction. The procedures of this dinner out with the important Fannings had been explained to the girls so many times in the last few days and particularly today that there really was no point in clowning around to get their mother to be more lenient.

"Mami, just please don't order anything I don't like, please?" Sandi pleaded. She had always been a fussy eater, and now that they had come to the States, it seemed as if there were twice as many inedible foods that could be piled high on her plate.

"No fish, Mami," Carla reminded her. "I get sick to my stomach."

126

"And nothing with mayonnaise," Yoyo added. "I can't eat—"

"Girls!" Their mother lifted up her hands like an Island traffic policeman, halting their requests. On her face was the panicked look she had worn ever since they had arrived in New York three months ago after a narrow escape from the secret police. At the least provocation, she would burst out crying, lose her temper, or threaten to end up in Bellevue, the place, she had learned, where crazy people were sent in this country.

"Can't you make a little effort tonight?" Her mother's voice was so sad that the youngest, Fifi, began to cry. "I don't want to go," she moaned. "I don't want to go."

"But why on earth not?" Mami asked, her face brightening. She seemed genuinely mystified, as if she hadn't terrorized them for days into thinking of this outing as equivalent to going to the doctor for their booster shots. "It's going to be such fun. The Fannings are taking us to a special Spanish restaurant that was written up in a magazine. You girls will like it, I'm sure. And there's going to be a floor show—"

"What's that?" Sandi, who had lost interest in pleading for a reasonable menu and had been fiddling with the ribbon in her hair, looked up. "Floor show?"

A playful expression came on their mother's face. She lifted her shoulders, curled her arms over head, and clapped her hands, then stamped her feet, fast, fast, fast, fast on the floor as if she were putting out a fire. "Flamenco dancing! ¡Olé! Remember the dancers?" Sandi nodded. They had all been enthralled by the folk dancers from Madrid at the Dominican World's Fair last year. As Mami began to explain that this restaurant had shows of Spanish dancers as well as yummy Spanish food, a series of thumps sounded on the floor from below.

The girls glanced at each other and looked towards their mother, who rolled her eyes. "La Bruja," she explained. "I forgot." The old woman in the apartment below, who had a helmet of beauty-parlor-blue hair, had been complaining to the super since the day the family moved in a few months ago. The Garcías should be evicted. Their food smelled. They spoke too loudly and not in English. The kids sounded like a herd of wild burros. The Puerto Rican super, Alfredo, came to their door almost daily. Could Mrs. García turn the radio down? Could Mrs. García maybe keep the girls more in line? The neighbor downstairs had been awakened by the clatter of their shoes on the floor.

"If I keep them any more in line," their mother began—and then Sandi heard her mother's voice breaking. "We have to walk around. We have to breathe."

Alfredo surveyed the fourth-floor lobby behind his back, then murmured under his breath. "I understand, I understand." He shrugged his shoulders, helpless. "It is a difficult place, this country, before you get used to it. You have to not take things personal." He brightened his voice at the end, but Sandi's mother merely nodded quietly.

"And how are my little señoritas?" Alfredo called over Mrs. García's shoulders. The girls forced smiles as they had been taught, but Sandi, in revenge, also crossed her eyes. She did not like Alfredo; something about the man's overfriendliness and his speaking to them in English even though they all knew Spanish made her feel uneasy. La Bruja downstairs, she thought of as the devil—her being below them made sense. When Sandi played Toro, bullfighting Yoyo with a towel, she would shout after each successful scrape with death, *¡Olé!* and stamp her feet in triumph, lifting her right hand to the crowd. She always had a bad conscience afterwards, but she couldn't help herself. One day soon after they had moved in, La Bruja had stopped her mother and the girls in the lobby and spat out that ugly word the kids at school sometimes used: "Spics! Go back to where you came from!"

As soon as Papi came home from his shift at the hospital, he showered, singing a favorite Island song that made the girls giggle as they slipped on their party dresses. They were already in a giddy mood from an inspired discovery that the Fannings' name sure sounded like the word for a person's bottom they had recently learned in the playground at school. "We're going to eat with the fannies," one sister would say to make the others laugh. Papi emerged from the bathroom combing his dark wet curls flat. He looked at the girls and winked. "Your Papi is a dashing man, eh?" He posed in front of the hall mirror, turning this way and that. "A handsome man, your Papi."

The girls indulged him with cries of "*Ay*, Papi." This was the first time in New York that they had seen their father in a lighthearted mood. Mostly he worried about *la situación* back home. Some uncles were in trouble. Tío Mundo had been jailed, and Tío Fideho was maybe dead. Papi had not been able to get an American doctor's license—some hitch about his foreign education—and the money was running out. Dr. Fanning was trying to help out by lining up jobs, but first Papi needed to pass his licensing exam. It had been Dr. Fanning who had arranged the fellowship that had allowed them all to get out of the old country. And now, the good doctor and his wife had invited the whole family out to an expensive restaurant in the city as a treat. The Fannings knew the Garcías could not afford such a luxury these days. They were such nice people, that was the truth, Mami said, they gave you hope that maybe at the bottom Americans were kind souls.

"But you must behave," Mami said, going back to the same old Epistle. "You must show them what a nice family you come from."

As Mami and Papi finished dressing, the girls watched, fussing at their tights, an uncomfortable new article of clothing. These things bunched at the ankles and sagged at the crotch so you always felt as if your pants might be falling down. They made you feel like those bandaged mummies in the museum. If you unwrapped them, Sandi had pondered, misting the glass case with her breath, would they still be dark Egyptians or would their skin have turned pale after such long bondage—like American skin under all these heavy clothes for the winter that was just starting?

Sandi leaned her elbows on the vanity and watched her mother comb her dark hair in the mirror. Tonight Mami was turning back into the beauty she had been back home. Her face was pale and tragic in the lamplight; her bright eyes shone like amber held up to the light. She wore a black dress with a scoop back and wide shoulders so her long neck had the appearance of a swan gliding on a lake. Around her neck sparkled her good necklace that had real diamonds. "If things get really bad," Mami sometimes joked grimly, "I'll sell the necklace and earrings Papito gave me." Papi always scowled and told her not to speak such nonsense.

If things ever get that bad, Sandi thought, she would sell her charm bracelet with the windmill that always got caught on her clothing. She would even cut her hair and sell it—a maid back home had told her that girls with good hair could always do that. She had no idea who would buy it. She had not seen hair for sale in the big department stores Mami sometimes took them through on outings "to see this new country." But Sandi would make the needed sacrifices. Tonight, she thought, with the rich Fannings, she would present herself as the daughter willing to make these sacrifices. Maybe they would adopt her, and give her an allowance like other American girls got, which Sandi would then pass on to her real family. Provided she could see them periodically, that would not be a bad life being an only child in a fine, rich, childless American family.

Downstairs, the doorman, Ralph, who had himself come from a country called Ireland as a boy, stood by the opened door and gave each young lady a sweeping bow as she passed by. He always flirted with the girls, calling them the Misses Garcías as if they were rich people's children. Mami often quipped that Ralph probably made more money than Papi on his fellowship. Thank God their grandfather was helping them out. "Without Papito," Mami confided in her girls, swearing them never to repeat this to their father, "without Papito, we would have to go on welfare." Welfare, they knew, was what people in this country got so they wouldn't turn into beggars like those outside La Catedral back home. It was Papito who paid the rent and bought them their winter clothes and spoiled them once with an outing to Lincoln Center to see the doll-like ballerinas dancing on their toes.

"Will you be needing a taxi tonight, Doc?" Ralph asked their father as he did every time the family came out all dressed up. Usually Papi said, "No, thank you, Ralph," and the family turned the corner and took a bus. Tonight, though, to Sandi's surprise, her father splurged. "Yes, please, Ralph, a Checker for all my girls." Sandi could not get over how happy her father seemed. She slipped her hand into his, and he gave it a squeeze before he released it. He was not a man to show public affection on foreign soil.

As the taxi sped along, Mami had to repeat the address for the driver because the man could not understand Papi's accent. Sandi realized with a pang one of the things that had been missing in the last few months. It was precisely this kind of special attention paid to them. At home there had always been a chauffeur opening a car door or a gardener tipping his hat and a half dozen maids and nursemaids acting as if the health and well-being of the de la Torre-García children were of wide public concern. Of course, it was usually the de la Torre boys, not the girls, who came in for special consideration. Still, as bearers of the de la Torre name, the girls were made to feel important.

The restaurant had a white awning with its name EL FLAMENCO in brilliant red letters. A doorman, dressed up as a dignitary with a flaming red band across his white ruffled shirt, opened the car door for them. A carpet on the sidewalk led into the reception foyer, from which they could see into a large room of tables dressed up with white tablecloths and napkins folded to look like bishops' hats. Silverware and glasses gleamed like ornaments. Around the occupied tables handsome waiters gathered, their black hair slicked back into bullfighters' little ponytails. They wore cummerbunds and white shirts with ruffles on the chest—beautiful men like the one Sandi would someday marry. Best of all were the rich, familiar smells of garlic and onion and the lilting cadence of Spanish spoken by the dark-eyed waiters, who reminded Sandi of her uncles.

At the entrance to the dinning room, the maître d' explained that Mrs. Fanning had called to say she and her husband were on their way, to go ahead and sit down and order some drinks. He led them, a procession of six, to a table right next to a platform. He pulled out all their chairs, handed them each an opened menu, then bowed and backed away. Three waiters descended on the table, filling water glasses, adjusting silverware and plates. Sandi sat very still and watched their beautiful long fingers fast at work.

"Something to drink, señor?" one of them said, addressing Papi.

"Can I have a Coke?" Fifi piped up, but then backed down when her mother and her sisters eyed her. "I'll have chocolate milk."

Their father laughed good-naturedly, aware of the waiting waiter. "I don't think they have chocolate milk. Cokes is fine for tonight. Right, Mami."

Mami rolled her eyes in mock exasperation. She was too beautiful tonight to be their mother and to impose the old rules. "Have you noticed?" she whispered to Papi when the waiter had left with the drink orders. The girls drew in to hear. Mami was the leader now that they lived in the States. *She* had gone to school in the States. *She* spoke English without a heavy accent. "Look at the menu. Notice how there aren't any prices? I bet a Coke here is a couple of dollars."

Sandi's mouth dropped open. "A couple of dollars!"

Her mother hushed her with an angry look. "Don't embarrass us, please, Sandi!" she said, and then laughed when Papi reminded her that Spanish was not a secret language in this place.

"*Ay,* Mami." He covered her hand briefly with his. "This is a special night. I want us to have a good time. We need a celebration."

"I suppose," Mami said, sighing. "And the Fannings are paying."

Papi's face tightened.

"There's nothing to be ashamed of," Mami reminded him. "When they were our guests back home, we treated them like royalty."

That was true. Sandi remembered when the famous Dr. Fanning and his wife had come down to instruct the country's leading doctors on new procedures for heart surgery. The tall, slender man and his goofy wife had been guests in the family compound. There had been many barbecues with the driveway lined with cars and a troop of chauffeurs under the palm trees exchanging news and gossip.

When the drinks arrived, Papi made a funny toast, in Spanish and loud enough for the waiters' benefit, but they were all too professional, and if they did overhear, no one chuckled. Just as they all lifted their glasses, Mami leaned into the table. "They're here." Sandi turned to see the maître d' heading in their direction with a tall, dressed-up woman,

and behind her, a towering, preoccupied-looking man. It took
a moment to register that these were the same human beings
who had loitered around the pool back on the Island, looking
silly in sunglasses and sunhats, noses smeared with suntan
cream, and speaking a grossly inadequate Spanish to the
maids.

A flutter of hellos and apologies ensued. Papi stood up,
and Sandi, not knowing what manners were called for, stood
up too, and was eyed by her mother to sit back down. The
doctor and his wife lingered over each girl, "trying to get them
straight," and remembering how each one had been only this
tall when last they had seen them. "What little beauties!" Dr.
Fanning teased. "Carlos, you've got quite a harem here!" The
four girls watched their father's naughty smile tilt on his face.

For the first few minutes the adults exchanged news.
Dr. Fanning told how he had spoken with a friend who was
the manager of an important hotel that needed a house doctor.
The job was a piece of cake, Dr. Fanning explained, mostly
keeping rich widows in Valium, but heck, the pay was good.
Sandi's father looked down at his plate, grateful, but also
embarrassed to be in such straits and to be so beholden.

The Fannings' drinks arrived. Mrs. Fanning drank
hers down in several greedy swallows, then ordered another.
She had been quiet during the flurry of arrival, but now she
gushed questions, raising her eyebrows and pulling long faces
when Mrs. García explained that they had not been able to
get any news from the family ever since the news blackout two
weeks back.

Sandi studied the woman carefully. Why had Dr. Fanning, who was tall and somewhat handsome, married this
plain, bucktoothed woman? Maybe she came from a good
family, which back home was the reason men married plain,
bucktoothed women. Maybe Mrs. Fanning came with all the
jewelry she had on, and Dr. Fanning had been attracted by
its glittering the way little fishes are if you wrap tinfoil on a
string and dangle it in the shallows.

Dr. Fanning opened his menu. "What would everyone
like? Girls?" This was the moment they had been so carefully
prepared for. Mami would order for them—they were not to
be so rude or forward as to volunteer a special like or dislike.
Besides, as Sandi tried reading the menu, with the help of her

index finger, sounding out syllables, she did not recognize the names of dishes listed.

Her mother explained to Dr. Fanning that she would order two *pastelónes* for the girls to share.

"Oh, but the seafood here is so good," the doctor pleaded, looking at her from above his glasses, which had slipped down on his nose like a schoolteacher's. "How about some paella, girls, or *camarones a la vinagreta?*"

"They don't eat shrimp," their mother said, and Sandi was grateful to her for defending them from this dreaded, wormy food. On the other hand, Sandi would have been glad to order something different and all to herself. But she remembered her mother's warnings.

"Mami," Fifi whispered, "what's *pastolone?*"

"*Pastelón*, Cuca." Mami explained it was a casserole like Chucha used to make back home with rice and ground beef. "It's very good. I know you girls will like it." Then she gave them a pointed look they understood to mean, they *must* like it.

"Yes," they said nicely when Dr. Fanning asked if *pastelón* was indeed what they wanted.

"Yes, what?" Mami coached.

"Yes, thank you," they chorused. The doctor laughed, then winked knowingly at them.

Their orders in and fresh drinks on the table, the grownups fell into the steady drone of adult conversation. Now and again the changed cadence of a story coming through made Sandi lean forward and listen. Otherwise, she sat quietly, playing with sugar packets until her mother made her stop. She watched the different tables around theirs. All the other guests were white and spoke in low, unexcited voices. Americans, for sure. They could have eaten anywhere, Sandi thought, and yet they had come to a *Spanish* place for dinner. La Bruja was wrong. Spanish was something other people paid to be around.

Her eye fell on a young waiter whose job seemed to be to pour water into the goblets at each table when they ran low. Every time she caught his eye, she would glance away embarrassed, but with boredom she grew bolder. She commenced a little flirtation; he smiled, and each time she smiled back, he approached with his silver pitcher to refill her water glass. Her mother noticed and said in coded scolding, "Their well is going to run dry."

In fact, Sandi had drunk so much water that, she explained quietly to Mami, she was going to have to go to the toilet. Her mother cast her another of her angry looks. They had been cautioned against making any demands tonight during dinner. Sandi squirmed at her seat, unwilling to go, unless she could be granted a smiling permission.

Papi offered to accompany her. "I could use the men's room myself." Mrs. Fanning also stood up and said she could stand to leave behind a little something. Dr. Fanning gave her a warning look, not too different from the one Sandi's mother had given her.

The three of them trooped to the back of the restaurant where the maître d' had directed, and down a narrow flight of stairs, lit gloomily by little lamps hung in archways. In the poorly lit basement Mrs. Fanning squinted at the writing on the two doors. *"Damas? Caballeros?"* Sandi checked an impulse to correct the American lady's pronunciation. "Hey there, Carlos, you're going to have to translate for me so I don't end up in the wrong room with you!" Mrs. Fanning rolled her hips in a droll way like someone trying to keep up a Hula Hoop.

Papi looked down at his feet. Sandi had noticed before that around American women he was not himself. He rounded his shoulders and was stiffly well mannered, like a servant. "Sandi will show you," he said, putting his daughter between himself and Mrs. Fanning, who laughed at his discomfort. "Go ahead then, sugar pie." Sandi held open the door marked DAMAS for the American lady. As Mrs. Fanning turned to follow, she leaned towards Sandi's father and brushed her lips on his.

Sandi didn't know whether to stand there foolishly or dash in and let the door fall on this uncomfortable moment. Like her father, she looked down at her feet, and waited for the giggling lady to sweep by her. Even in the dimly lit room, Sandi could see her father's face darken with color.

Sandi and Mrs. Fanning found themselves in a pretty little parlor with a couch and lamps and a stack of perfumed towels. Sandi spied the stalls in an adjoining room and hurried into one, releasing her bladder. Relieved, she now felt the full and shocking weight of what she had just witnessed. A married American woman kissing her father!

As she let herself out of her stall, she heard Mrs. Fanning still active in hers. Quickly, she finished hitching up her silly tights, then swished her hands under the faucet, beginning to dry them on her dress, but remembering after an initial swipe, the towels. She took one from the stack, wiped her hands, and tapped at her face as she had seen Mami do with the powder puff. Looking at herself in the mirror, she was surprised to find a pretty girl looking back at her. It was a girl who could pass as American, with soft blue eyes and fair skin, looks that were traced back to a great-great-grandmother from Sweden at every family gathering. She lifted her bangs—her face was delicate like a ballerina's. It struck her impersonally as if it were a judgment someone else was delivering, someone American and important, like Dr. Fanning: she was pretty. She had heard it said before, of course, but the compliment was always a group compliment to all the sisters, so Sandi thought this was a politeness friends of her parents said about daughters just as they tended to say, "They're so big" or "They're so smart" about sons. Being pretty, she would not have to go back to where she came from. Pretty spoke both languages. Pretty belonged in this country to spite La Bruja. As she studied herself, the stall door behind her opened in the mirror. Sandi let her bangs fall and rushed out of the room.

Her father was waiting in the anteroom, pacing nervously, his hands worrying the change in his pocket. "Where is she?" he whispered.

Sandi pointed back in the room with her chin.

"That woman is drunk," he whispered, crouching down beside Sandi. "But I can't insult her, imagine, our one chance in this country." He spoke in the serious, hushed voice he had used with Mami those last few days in the old country. "*Por favor*, Sandi, you're a big girl now. Not a word of this to your mother. You know how she is these days."

Sandi eyed him. This was the first time her father had ever asked her to do something sneaky. Before she had time to respond, the bathroom door swung open. Her father stood up. Mrs. Fanning called out, "Why, here you are, sugar!"

"Yes, here we are!" her father said in a too cheerful

voice. "And we must better get back to the table before they send the marines!" He smiled archly, as if he had just thought up this quip he had been making for weeks.

Mrs. Fanning threw her head back and laughed. "Oh, Carlos!"

Her father joined the American lady's phony laughter, then stopped abruptly when he noticed Sandi's eyes on him. "What are you waiting for?" He spoke in a stern voice, nodding towards the stairs. Sandi glanced away, hurt. Mrs. Fanning laughed again and led the way up the narrow winding stairs. It was like coming up out of a dungeon, Sandi decided. She would tell her sisters this and make them wish they had gone to the bathroom as well, though truly, Sandi wished she had herself never strayed from the table. She wouldn't have seen what she could not now hope to forget.

At the table, the young waiter tucked the chair in for her. He was still lovely, his skin so smooth and of a rich olive color, his hands long and slender like those of angels in illustrations, holding their choir books. But this man could very well lean forward just as Mrs. Fanning had done downstairs. He could try to kiss *her*, Sandi, on the lips. She did not let her glance fall in his direction again.

Instead, she studied the Fannings intently for clues as to their mysterious behavior. One thing she noticed was that Mrs. Fanning drank a lot of wine, and each time she nodded to the waiter to fill her glass, Dr. Fanning said something to her out of the corner of his mouth. At one point when the waiter leaned toward her empty glass, Dr. Fanning covered it with his hand. "That's enough," he snapped, and quickly the waiter leaned away again.

"What a party fart," Mrs. Fanning observed, loud enough for the table to hear, though "fart" was not a word the girls recognized. Mami instantly began to fuss at Sandi and her sisters, pretending that the exchange of angry whispering between the Fannings was not taking place. But little Fifi could not be distracted from the scene at the end of the table: she stared wide-eyed at the bickering Fannings, and then over at Mami with a serious look of oncoming tears. Mami winked at her, and smiled a high-watt smile to reassure the little girl that these Americans need not be taken seriously.

Blessedly, their platters of food appeared, borne by a

cortege of waiters, directed by the busybody maître d'. The tension dispelled as the two couples took small, pensive bites of their different servings. Compliments and evaluations erupted all around the table. Sandi found most of the things on her plate inedible. But there was a generous decorative lettuce leaf under which much of the goopy meat and greasy rice could be tucked away.

Tonight she felt beyond either of her parents: she could tell that they were small people compared to these Fannings. She had herself witnessed a scene whose disclosure could cause trouble. What did she care if her parents demanded that she eat all of her *pastelón*? She would say, just as an American girl might, "I don't wanna. You can't make me. This is a free country."

"Sandi, look!" It was her father, trying to befriend her. He was pointing towards the stage where the lights were dimming. Six señoritas in long, fitted dresses with flaring skirts and maracas in their hands flounced onto the stage. The guitarist came on and strummed a summoning tune. Beautiful men in toreador outfits joined their ladies. They stamped their feet for hello, and the ladies stamped back, Hello! Six and six, *damas* and *caballeros*, they went through a complicated series of steps, the women's maracas clacking a teasing beat, the men echoing their partners' moves with sultry struts, and foot stomps. These were not the dainty and chaste twirls and curtseys of the ballerinas at Lincoln Center. These women looked, well—Sandi knew no other way to put it—they looked as if they wanted to take their clothes off in front of the men.

Yoyo and Fifi were closest to the stage, but Mami let Carla and Sandi pull their chairs around in a cluster and join their sisters. The dancers clapped and strutted, tossing their heads boldly like horses. Sandi's heart soared. This wild and beautiful dance came from people like her, Spanish people, who danced the strange, disquieting joy that sometimes made Sandi squeeze Fifi's hand hard until she cried or bullfight Yoyo with a towel until both girls fell in a giggling, exhausted heap on the floor that made La Bruja beat her ceiling with a broom handle.

"The girls are having such fun," she heard her mother confide to Mrs. Fanning.

"Me too," the American lady observed. "These guys are something else. Hey, Lori, watch that one's tight tights."

"Very nice," Sandi's mother said a little stiffly.

Dr. Fanning hissed at his wife. "That's enough, Sylvia."

As the show progressed, Sandi could see that the dancers' faces were becoming beaded with sweat. Wet patches spread under their arms, and their smiles were strained. Still they were beautiful as first one couple, then another, came forward in solo dances. Then the men withdrew, and from somewhere they acquired roses, which they presented to their partners. The women began a dance in which the roses were held in their mouths, and their maracas clacked a merciless thank you to the men.

Behind Sandi, a chair scraped the floor, another fell over, and two figures hurled by. It was Mrs. Fanning, with Dr. Fanning giving chase! She scrambled up onto the platform, clapping her hands over her head, Dr. Fanning lunging at but missing her as she escaped onto center stage. The dancers good-naturedly made way. Dr. Fanning did not follow, but with an angry shrug of his shoulders, headed back to their table.

"Let her enjoy herself," Sandi's mother said. Her voice was full of phony good cheer. "She is just having a good time."

"She's had too much to drink is what she's had," the doctor snapped.

The restaurant came alive with the American lady's clowning. She was a good ham, bumping her hips up against the male dancers and rolling her eyes. The diners laughed and clapped. The management, sensing a good moment, gave her a spotlight, and the guitarist came forward, strumming a popular American tune with a Spanish flair. One of the male dancers partnered Mrs. Fanning—who advanced as the dancer withdrew in a pantomine of a cartoon chase. The diners roared their approval.

All but Sandi. Mrs. Fanning had broken the spell of the wild and beautiful dancers. Sandi could not bear to watch her. She turned her chair around to face the table and occupied herself with her water glass, twisting the stem around, making damp links on the white cloth.

To a round of applause, Mrs. Fanning was escorted

back to the table by her partner. Sandi's father stood up and pulled her chair out for her.

"Let's go." Dr. Fanning turned, looking for the waiter to ask for the check.

"Ah, come on, sugar, loosen up, will ya?" his wife coaxed him. One of the dancers had given the American lady her rose, and Mrs. Fanning now tried to stick it in her husband's lapel. Dr. Fanning narrowed his eyes at her, but before he could speak, the table was presented with a complimentary bottle of champagne from the management. As the cork popped, a few of the customers in adjoining tables applauded and lifted their glasses up in a toast to Mrs. Fanning.

"A toast to all of us!" Mrs. Fanning held up her glass. "Come on, girls," she urged them. Sandi's sisters lifted their water glasses and clinked the American lady's.

"Sandi!" her mother said. "You too."

Reluctantly, Sandi lifted her glass.

Dr. Fanning held up his glass and tried to inject a pointed seriousness into the moment: "To you, the Garcías. Welcome to this country." Now her parents lifted their glasses, and in her father's eyes, Sandi noted gratitude, and in her mother's eyes, a moistness that meant barely checked tears.

As Dr. Fanning spoke to one of the waiters, a dancer approached the table, carrying a large straw basket with a strap that went around her neck. She tipped the basket towards the girls and smiled a wide, warm smile at the two men. Inside the basket were a dozen dark-haired Barbie dolls dressed like Spanish señoritas. The dancer held up a doll and puffed out the skirt of its dress so that it opened prettily like a fully blown flower.

"Would you like one?" she asked little Fifi. The woman spoke in English, but her voice was heavily accented like Dr. García's.

Fifi nodded eagerly, then looked over at her mother, who was eyeing the little girl. Slowly Fifi shook her head. "No?" the dancer said in a surprised voice, lifting up her eyebrows. She looked at the other girls, her eye falling on Sandi. "You would like one?"

Sandi, of course, remembered the much-repeated caution to the girls that they should not ask for any special dishes or treats of any sort. The Garcías could not afford extras, and they did not want to put their hosts in the embarrassing position of having to spend money out of largesse. Sandi stared at the small doll. She was a perfect replica of the beautiful dancers, dressed in a long, glittery gown with a pretty tortoiseshell comb in her hair, from which cascaded a tiny, lacy mantilla. On her feet were strapped tiny black heels such as the dancers had worn. Sandi ignored her mother's fierce look and reached out for the doll.

With the tip of her painted fingernail, the dancer salesgirl showed the miniature maracas the doll was holding. Sandi felt such tenderness as when a new mother uncurls the tiny fists of a newborn. She turned to her father, ignoring her mother's glare. "Papi, can I have her?" Her father looked up at the pretty salesgirl and smiled. Sandi could tell he wanted to make an impression. "Sure," he nodded, adding, "Anything for my girl." The salesgirl smiled.

Instantly the cry from the other three: "Me too, Papi! Me too!"

Her mother reached over and took the doll from Sandi's hands. "Absolutely not, girls." She shook her head at the dancer, who had since reached in her basket and extracted three more dolls.

Meanwhile the check had been brought, and Dr. Fanning was reviewing the items, stacking bills on a little tray. As he did so, Papi gazed down at the tablecloth. Back in the old country, everyone fought for the honor of paying. But what could he do in this new country where he did not even know if he had enough cash in his pocket to make good on buying the four dolls that he was now committed to provide for his girls.

"You know the rules!" Mami hissed at them.

"Please, Mami, please," Fifi begged, not understanding that the woman's offer of a doll did not mean they were free.

"No!" Mami said sharply. "And no more discussion, girls." The edge on her voice made Mrs. Fanning, who had been absently collecting her things, look up. "What's going on?" she asked the girls' mother. "Nothing," Mami said, and smiled tensely.

Sandi was not going to miss her chance. This woman had kissed her father. This woman had ruined the act of the beautiful dancers. The way Sandi saw it, this woman owed her something. "We want one of those dolls." Sandi pointed to the basket in which the dancer was rearranging the rejected dolls.

"Sandi!" her mother cried.

"Why, I think that's a swell idea! A souvenir!" Mrs. Fanning motioned the dancer back, who approached the table with her full cargo. "Give each of these girls a doll and put it on the bill. Sugar"—she turned to her husband, who had finished clapping the small folder closed—"hold your horses."

"I will not permit—" Papi sat forward, reaching in his back pocket for his wallet.

"Nonsense!" Mrs. Fanning hushed him. She touched his hand to prevent him from opening his wallet.

Papi flinched and then tried to disguise his reaction by pretending to shake her hand away. "I pay this."

"Don't take his money," Mrs. Fanning ordered the dancer, who smiled noncommittedly.

"Hey," Dr. Fanning said, agreeing with his wife. "We wanted to get the girls something, but heck, we didn't know what. This is perfect." He peeled four more tens from his wad. Papi exchanged a helpless look with Mami.

While her sisters fussed over which of the dolls to choose, Sandi grabbed the one dressed exactly like the dancers in the floor show. She stood the Barbie on the table and raised one of the doll's arms and pulled the other out so that the doll was frozen in the pose of the Spanish dancers.

"You are much too kind," her mother said to Mrs. Fanning, and then in a hard voice with the promise of later punishment, she addressed the four girls. "What do you say?"

"Thank you," Sandi's sisters chorused.

"Sandi?" her mother said.

Sandi looked up. Her mother's eyes were dark and beautiful like those of the little dancer before her. "Yes, Mami?" she asked politely, as if she hadn't heard the order.

"What do you say to Mrs. Fanning?"

Sandi turned to the woman whose blurry, alcoholic eyes and ironic smile intimated the things Sandi was just beginning to learn, things that the dancers knew all about, which was why they danced with such vehemence, such passion. She hopped her dancer right up to the American lady and gave her a bow. Mrs. Fanning giggled and returned an answering nod. Sandi did not stop. She pushed her doll closer, so that Mrs. Fanning aped a surprised, cross-eyed look. Holding her new doll right up to the American woman's face and tipping it so that its little head touched the woman's flushed cheek, Sandi made a smacking sound.

"*Gracias*," Sandi said, as if the Barbie doll had to be true to her Spanish costume.

CALL ME BARBIE

FOR DENISE

Gregg Shapiro

When my mother bought me a Ken doll,
my Aunt Darlene almost had a stroke.
Years later, she forbade my cousin Joel
to talk to me. My father said it was
because I was always badmouthing the family.
I think it was because I kissed my male
friends hello, wore Salvation Army clothes
and let Ken kiss my cousin's GI Joe.

I learned to braid hair on my sister
Dana's Barbie doll. None of her friends'
brothers could make a pigtail so tight,
not a strand of synthetic hair out of place.
I organized fashion shoots, gynecological
exams, and shopping sprees for her dolls.
My sister never complained. She had an older
brother who wanted to be her older sister.

My boyfriend's name is Ken. Even though
he doesn't have plastic-injection-molded
hair, I love him anyway. He has perfect
teeth, a deep voice, green eyes, and genitals
that leave nothing to the imagination.
Look, I even shaved my chest, just to make us
a more perfect match. As soon as I get used
to walking on my toes, you can call me Barbie.

TRIANGLES

Cathryn Hankla

We found her face down in the sand, one slightly bent arm extended over her head, one arm at her side, as if swimming. She wore a small wedge of polyester, and her hair felt sticky from salt water. I don't remember which one of us first spotted her, which one turned her bright blue eyes into the sun. Her perfectly applied blue eyeshadow had not smeared or run when she journeyed through the surf. You wore a black one-piece and carried Barbie on your palm. I wore a two-piece that I was constantly tugging up or down.

"Some little girl will be unhappy," I said.

You would be forty on your next birthday. "But we found her," you said.

I followed you back to our striped towels.

Barbie sits between us, knees bent, casting no shadow, and we cannot resist undressing her beneath the umbrella.

"She's smooth," I say. "As always."

You stare at her thighs, her arms, between her legs. "She never has to shave," you say sadly.

"When I played Barbie I always cut off her hair. My Barbie needed a set of wigs."

"She never started her period," you say. "She lives in the eternal present."

"This is depressing."

You stare into our naked Barbie's unblinking eyes.

"I'm thirsty—I'll get beers." I leave you holding her.

A-rattle with beer cans and ice, the cooler bangs against my legs, against yesterday's fresh bruises, as I struggle across the scorching sand to our oasis of shade. I see you far away, in the water, dipping beneath a wave.

Barbie's dirty pink stretch suit marks the place on the towel where she is missing. I plop down in her place, pop a top, and slurp the brew. I don my straw hat and bifocal sunglasses. I rub my hand over the callus of my heels which smoothes day by day as I scoot barefoot.

You seem to be drifting out, but you look comfortable floating on your back. I can see your full breasts bob above the waves, and then I see Barbie perched there on your chest, legs stuffed between your boobs, pert as the day she was formed.

I shut my eyes and pour beer down my throat.

I feel a touch of water on my shoulder. I look up and try to focus on Barbie's nippleless boobies. "I'm drunk."

"The water's perfect." You move to reach into the cooler.

I watch as you open a beer and raise it to drink. Water drips from the seat of your suit, and beer drips down your chin. I stand up and grab Barbie from between your breasts. "Ouch!"

"Sorry. But you looked ridiculous."

"Who cares? I was having fun." You drain your beer, stopping only to breathe and glare at me. I'm dressing Barbie in her tiny little swimsuit. I get her arranged on the towel, stomach down, in a modest position for sunning.

You pull your chair away, sit down with your book without speaking.

After half an hour has passed without our speaking, I say, "Barbie and I miss you."

You look up from your romance novel. "Oh, really?"

"Yes."

"How much?"

"We were wondering if you felt like going in for a while."

"I've been."

I get up from the towel with Barbie, walk toward you,

and hand her over. You take her into your hands and unsnap
the one snap at the back of her suit.

"I meant in the house," I say.

"Can Barbie come?"

I giggle. "Who knows?"

We drive toward the shore with Barbie straddling the dash.
Most of the time she takes the curves well, but occasionally
she tilts to one side or the other and I have to set her straight.
It has been three years since we found her and now she has a
full wardrobe: a new beach outfit complete with sunglasses, a
beach ball, Frisbee, and a towel of her own; a strapless sun-
dress with matching white sandals of the one-strap Barbie
variety; a brush and comb set; a French poodle and poodle
skirt; an apron and chef hat; a cardboard Dream House; a
motorcycle; a ski-party ensemble with neon jumpsuit and
parka; and a mink coat with Russian hat that we haven't
packed for this trip.

Two or three days pass, and we are becoming accus-
tomed to the routine of rising late, slightly hung over from
wine the night before, eating too much breakfast, and dragging
chairs, towels, kites, drinks, and Barbie down to the beach
for the day, when one morning it rains. And the phone rings.

You answer and immediately your voice sounds odd. I
leave the room. I wish the sun were out so I could just walk
down to the beach while you talk.

I decide to walk down to the beach anyway. The rain
isn't that hard or cold. But I'm feeling lazy, so I sit down on
the walkway, in view of the house, and wait, looking out at
the choppy, dull gray ocean. A pelican patrol moves slowly
along and I watch them dive for fish. After a while, a little
streak of sun shatters the dark horizon. And I sit there until
the clouds break up.

The week passes, a bit awkwardly but warm. We're out all
day long, soaking up sun, growing dark, plump from beer and
snacks. Every day you talk on the phone. The last night we're
sitting at supper, slowly tasting the feast of softshell crab and
shrimp we've prepared.

"I have something for you," you say. You leave the table, and return with a rectangular box.

I set down my fork to open the present. I tear a corner of the wrap and then pull the paper off in a ragged strip. I already know what it is. My stomach sinks and a pain pins my heart. I can't look at him through the cellophane. I set the box down and gaze across the table.

"It's Ken," you say. "I thought it'd be funny to get her a boyfriend." You look me straight in the eye as if this is the most normal thing in the world.

I keep my voice light. "Why?"

"Because he's her type."

"You mean he's plastic, too. And his head's hollow."

"Don't be mean," you say. "I can take him back if you don't like him."

"I don't think that's possible," I say.

I throw my shorts and shirts into the suitcase, and wad up my swimsuits and towels still wet from the line. I don't care if they mildew. I grab my beach chair and fling it into the trunk without wiping the crust of sand from its frame. I'm turning around in the driveway when I remember her. It ruins my exit, but I have to go back. I knock on the door.

When you answer, I say, "I want her."

"I found her, she's mine." You slam the door for effect, but it's not locked, so I follow you into the kitchen.

"Where is she?"

"You can't leave me here without a car."

"Keep the Barbie scooter." I am serious.

And then I see her on the table, back to back with Ken, in perfect balance.

"How long has she been seeing him?" I ask.

"A year."

I look at Ken's white tennis outfit, the maroon and dark blue banded neck and cuffs of his sport sweater, his stiff, matching shorts. His flat rubber tennis shoes angle straight up into the air. He's staring in the opposite direction, back into the kitchen, while Barbie stares out the window at the ocean.

"He's perfect for her," I say.

I leave her there.

BAR BARBIE

Wayne E. Kline

The band hasn't started playing yet and already she's barking requests. It goes like this: they're checkin' the mikes and here comes this wintry thing with a neck like a giraffe and an "undo my poise" attitude. Maybe it's her smile. Maybe it's the way she carries her purse, gartered to her fishnetted thigh. Maybe the night has ended, and flowers are all we see.

Faster than a number one best-seller she hits the floor, dancing a craze from the Indies, oblivious to the side-stricken laughter from the corns. What do they know about style, about dolls? . . . When someone comes up, she asks for a drink, something they could buy. Maybe that or a Rolls, the pink convertible one that moves like a paperweight down an icy chute, one gear forward and all the options of a larger space.

Eyes closed. So hard when they're painted on. She has to hold her hands in front, pushing patrons aside as she staggers to the ladies' room. Her rooted hair and all-vinyl skin come complete; there is little touch-up to do, maybe brown the complexion with some milk chocolate and a rag. When she comes out she is another person, astride an angora goat and spouting the accumulated gossip of a quilters' bee. Only the band recognizes her; before the show they guessed her weight.

• • •

There is this guy named Ken. He plays keyboards and is a
look-alike for himself. He is not pouty but has that expression
like he's always emerging from under the hood of a transporta-
tion product. Think of it this way: he was introduced to Barbie
at the beginning of his career, and now he thinks of nothing
else. This has been going on for thirty years. When he goes to
bed at night he lights a candle, like setting fire to somebody
else's jacket. "Barbie," he whispers, "Barbette."

It is closing time and lightning perforates the sky. Barbie has
to choose who to say good-bye to, and who to live with forever.
The club manager wants her hand, he wants her mind, her
ceaseless intellect. And there is Ken, who plays her like a
competitive event, with no limits or rules. When she looks into
his eyes, she feels as though he is an uncle, or son, or ideal
sex god of her era.

The lights go down like edges of a dream. Herr Ken-boy on
her lips, and how he kisses, as if educated by plumbers! And
his hands, so firm, like the ribs of a mold, shaping her to his
need. But the manager, awake in his shamed palace of flings,
signs to his bouncers, gnashes his scar-worn teeth like a kid left
out of holiday. For tomorrow, forever, for Barbie, entrance is
barred.

BARBIE & KEN, KEN & BARBIE

Philip Levine

Ken has a big job at Castle Air Force Base
where the work is challenging and the future
lies on the cutting room table, docile and clear
for Ken, who with scissors unwrinkles its face.

Ken drives to Paso Robles on the weekend
in a sports car that runs on needle bearings;
he takes the turns hard and as he does he sings
for up ahead is the ocean and the sand

and Barbie in a pink negligee, Barbie
waiting in her tall pink pumps, golf clubs ready.
The coast hills are greener than they used to be,
the ocean restless, only Ken is steady.

Soon they'll be together, brother and sister,
Barbie and Ken, sharing a toothbrush, sharing
a toilet, a tub, sharing the same old song
that freezes on their lips, sharing each other

for that breathless moment when the elders
bow to their credit card. Sundays would be hell
what with packing, parting, and the long haul
if brother and sister weren't such good soldiers.

BARBIE COMES OUT

Rebecca Brown

It's Saturday night at the Rose, our local girls' bar. I've parked myself at Pat's and my regular table— midway between the door and the bar. I'm nursing a schooner of Ballard Bitter and waiting for my best buddy to show. We usually meet here about eight to complain to each other about how shitty our work week was, the terrible paucity of romance in our lives, and the generally crappy state of the world. Pat and I have been dressing each others' wounds for years—we both have a propensity for stepping on the land mines of love. We've also tried, with much less success, to matchmake for each other. Steer each other to women we think are cute, safe, and relatively unpsychotic. Pat goes for the trad femme type: long hair, heels, purse, makeup, the works. I prefer a gal with a little muscle. This means, of course, that we're never in competition; we are comrades.

It's getting on about 8:15, and having sat here only a quarter of an hour eyeing a bar full of either seriously ensconced, disgustingly cutesy baby dyke couples, or steely, Tiparillo-puffing, lonely, old-style bar dykes, I'm getting discouraged enough to suggest to Pat, when she arrives, that we bag the girl watching for the evening and catch a movie at the Broadway. There's a Fred-and-Ginger double bill that I'm sure would cheer us up. More than once Pat and I have gotten ludicrously teary-eyed over F and G, knowing that the kind of romance that those two swung around with is no more.

I drape my jacket over my chair and a copy of SGN over hers to stake the place, and go to call her. I want to catch her before she leaves and suggest we meet at the theater instead. I get her machine: "Yo, Bart (her last name is Barton). Brown here. You there? Pick up the phone if you are. . . . Okay . . . I guess you're on your way to the Rose. See ya in a flash." I hang up and go back to the table.

I keep my eye on the door even more so I can catch her the second she arrives and steer her off to the flicks before she can place an order. When the door opens next, though, it isn't her, but it is exactly, precisely, breath-stoppingly what she would like to see on her plate. My gonads skip a vicarious beat for Pat. And I hear—I swear to God, I hear it as clear as if it were a real live human voice—the voice of the goddess, or fate, or my subconscious calling my name: Brown! Rebecca Brown! I recognize this as a little help, as if I needed some, to direct me to this female I am meant to acquire for Pat. The girl is a—there is no other word for it—*doll.*

The bar is smoky and getting packed. I do a wide mean glare around to let everyone know they shouldn't even think of moving in on the table while I'm gone. I push my way towards the door to nab the girl before she can slip away. I don't have to be so quick, though; she isn't moving at all. She's standing mute and still, telltale signs that this is her first time in a dyke bar. I practically rub my hands together with glee thinking how much Pat will enjoy showing this baby the town. But the closer I get, the less thick the wall of smoke between us is, the more I see she looks a little weird. She's standing so still her torso doesn't move. It almost looks like she isn't even breathing. The only thing that moves is her head, and it doesn't go up and down, just left and right as smoothly as a well-oiled hinge on a perfectly balanced door. Her hair is long, the way Pat likes, but so stiff if looks, if not an actual wig, at least sprayed beyond Brillo with industrial-strength mousse. And she's balancing on these astonishingly engineered high heels. She looks like a kid playing dress-up for the first time, or like some poor old lunk of a trans trying to squeeze into a pair of stretched-out triple-wides. She's got a purse, all right—one of those clutch jobs I have never seen for real in my whole life, but only in fact know about from Perry Mason reruns.

I step up closer. Her makeup is smooth. Her skin is utterly flawless. Perfect. Eerily perfect.

Then all of the sudden I get it: this poor kid is one of those desperate out-of-towners who's come to Seattle for a last chance at the Fred Hutchinson Cancer Center (only a few blocks away). She's probably on chemo (hence the wig, the skin) and my heart breaks for her.

Whether she's just stumbled into the Rose by mistake or whether she has sought out this bar particularly, I don't care. I just know that I feel so sad for her, I'm going to be extra nice. And Pat will be, too, when she gets here. We'll take this dear girl under our wing and show her as much of the town as she can stand—the Space Needle, the Market, the Locks, the Sound. We'll take her for a ferry ride, maybe go up to the islands. We'll buy her ice cream sundaes and we'll take her to the movies. We'll be the best Good Samaritan duo anyone could ask for.

I don't want to startle her so I try to casually catch her eye and give her an open smile. But her eyes don't move. She seems like she can only stare straight forward. So I go right up to her. I try to sound nice. Not *too* nice, just decently nice.

"Hi!" I smile my office-temp smile. "You need a place to sit? I'm waiting for my friend, so there's a free chair at my table."

She turns her head to face me. Smooth. No dip. Her eyes are this bizarre pastel blue. I wonder if they're contacts, to cover up some horrible side effect of her meds. She doesn't blink. Her mouth is pooched in a fixed stage-fright smile.

"Thank you!" she says. As clipped as someone who's only ever spoken in a language lab.

Poor thing's so nervous!

"I'm just over here." I point to the table and she takes a step. Her left foot and leg swing forward perfectly straight, like the Little Tin Soldier. Then her right. Her knees don't bend. Her high heels scrape across the floor like a clumsy cross-country skier. The crowd parts around her. (We're very sensitive to differently abled people in our community.) Everyone tries to pretend they don't notice her, but everybody tries to sneak a peek. I follow her as unruffled as I can. She bends from the waist, straight as a can opener, to pull the chair out. Her back doesn't curve. She tries to pull the chair out, but her fingers won't curl.

Is she deformed as well? Got some hideous paralysis? My heart breaks into even smaller pieces for her. I scoot up and discreetly pull the chair out for her. It's always tricky: some of the time they're pissed off that you have demeaned them by trying to help; some of the time they're pissed off that you don't offer to help; but some of the time you do okay. Like this time. I pull the chair out. She chirps, "Thank you!" and her butt falls towards the chair. I catch her and lower her carefuly. She's so rigid! When she lands I hear this huge crack and think, Dear Christ, I've broken her something-or-other. I don't know whether to hold on or let go.

"Thank you!" she chirps again. Exactly the same. Like a tape.

"You're welcome," I say, and plop into my chair across from her. "It might take a while for the waitron to get to us. You want me to get you something from the bar?" I hoist my empty schooner up. "I could use a refill myself."

"Thank you!" she says, exactly the very same. Then a pause. "But no thank you!"

"Oh . . . okay."

Then I lean over to her real close, so no one else can hear. I don't want to embarrass her. "Look, if it's the cash, I can spring for you. My treat. And no . . . uh . . . obligation." Though as soon as I say "obligation," I realize she has no idea what kind of thing I could mean. Bless her heart.

She doesn't say anything.

"Soda," I say, "juice, herb tea?" She's probably on one of those low-everything diets.

"Thank you." Pause. "But no thank you!"

"Well . . . I'm gonna get something myself. Be right back." I take my glass up to the bar, get another bitter for me and a Calistoga for her, just in case. I go to the phone and call Pat again. Her machine. "Pat. Me again. Hey, get yer ass down here. We've got a social service project on our hands. And you'll think she's cute. See ya pronto."

When I get back to the table she hasn't moved at all.

I slide the Calistoga over to her and smile. "In case you change your mind."

"Thank you!"

She's starting to walk the line with this one.

I lean back in my chair. "I just called my pal Pat. She should be here soon. She's terrific." All this to lay on really thick that I'm not trying to hit on her.

She still doesn't say anything. Chatty Cathy, this one ain't.

I'm fumbling around for a direction in which to lead this scintillating dialogue when she says, "I'm waiting for a friend too. My friend is flying in from Colorado."

She says "friend" that nervous, non-gender-specific way closet cases do. She doesn't fool me. For chrissake, we're in the Lesbian bar.

"I'll keep an eye out," I say casually. "What's your 'friend' look like."

This puts her on the spot. Her flat blue eyes stare in front of her. She doesn't blink. Then somehow I see something like panic rising in them. I wonder if she's making this "friend" up. I change the topic.

"By the way—" I stick my hand out "—I'm Rebecca."

"I'm—" She clears her throat. It takes her a while to get it out, like she's trying it on for the first time. "I'm Barbara." And her right arm springs up. Her elbow doesn't bend, just sticks straight out. She knocks into my beer. I catch it before it spills and take her hand. Her skin is smooth, no lines at all. Cool. Hairless. It feels a little creepy, to tell the truth. I shake her hand slowly, more like sawing up and down. Her fingers don't bend at all.

"Nice to meet you," I say.

"Thank you!"

If she says that again, I'll scream.

"You new in town, Barb?"

She doesn't like that. One bit.

"That's Barbara," she snaps.

Maybe she does have a little bite. "Sorry," I mumble. "Barbara. So, you new in town?"

She hesitates. "Somewhat."

Maybe she's been here for treatment before. "Where you from?"

"Made in America."

Ha, I think. "Me too," I say as coolly as I can. "Where-abouts?"

Long pause. "Many places."

"Military brat?"

"Sometimes."

"Sometimes?"

"Sometimes not."

I can't tell if she's unbearably shy, uncomfortable as hell, or something of a tease. In any case this is probably not going to be the sparkling conversation one would like to think occurs in this cosmopolitan watering hole of the alienated-affection elite of King County. More like the excruciatingly polite question-and-answer format one conducts with extremely vapid, though often dangerously cute, daughters of difficult bosses. But this one isn't a bimbo—just strange. I still feel sorry for her and all, but I do wish she'd try a little.

"I didn't catch your friend's name."

She catches her breath and makes this horrible gagging "-ck-ck-ck" sound in the back of her throat and I think she's going to choke and die. I leap up and hope I can remember the Heimlich maneuver. Patricia, where are you? (She's a doc.) But then Barbara catches her breath and sounds okay. Thank God.

"Eh—" she sniffs. "Eh . . . hi . . . her . . . name . . . my friend's name . . ." She sobs.

"Hey, it's okay," I say. If it's that hard for her to admit her "friend" is female, I'm not going to force her. I lean over and pat her forearm. Smooth and chilly. I shiver, but try to sound nice when I say, "It's okay, It's okay."

I think she's trying to nod her head to say thanks, but all she can do is swing it left and right. She sniffs.

"You want to tell me something about your friend?"

She turns her head left and right again: Yes? No? Christ, I can't tell.

"There, there," I say, patting the air above her arm (I don't want to touch it again). I feel a tear drop on my skin. She sniffles a great big one. Then jerks her arm into her purse and saws back and forth until she pulls out a tissue. Her shoulder does this amazing wrench when she pulls the tissue up. She honks into her hankie. I look away discreetly. When I look back her makeup is running. Blue smears down her cheeks. She daubs her hankie around her eyes. Rubs her eyes.

All of which is fine and normal for a femme. Except when she pulls the tissue away from her eyes and honks into it again, and I get that chance to look again at her eyes, I gasp. It isn't just that she's rubbed her mascara off—she's also rubbed off her eyes. Below her forehead, above her nose, there's only a blue-black smudge.

Then it's my turn to make that gagging "-*ck-ck-ck*" sound. I think I'm gonna be sick. I close my eyes and tell myself my beer must have been spiked. I wrap my hands around my glass and count to ten. When I open my eyes again her eyes are still gone. I look around to see how everyone else is reacting to this. But everyone else—for once—is minding her own business. I carefully look back at Barbara's face. Her eyes are adios.

Though evidently not for the first time. Because Barbara's not flustered at all. She roots around in her purse again and pulls out a tube of mascara and a compact. It's painful to watch her struggle to open the compact with those fingers, but not as weird as watching her eyeless face. Part of me wants to reach over and open the compact for her, but part of me doesn't want to admit what I'm seeing. She pops the compact open, sets it on the table, opens the mascara—or eyeliner or whatever the hell it is; God knows I've never used any of that shit—and stretches her forehead up. She faces the compact mirror, as if she could actually see. She sniffs quietly, with dignity, as she reapplies herself. She twirls her eyelashes into shape and makes the thin arched line of her eyebrows. She extracts some teeny jars from her purse, unscrews the lids, and lines them up in a row. She folds her whole left hand at an angle so she can dip her pinkie in. She daubs her pinkie to her face and makes two tidy ovals of white. She rolls her pinkie in the Kleenex to clean it. Then dips her right pinkie into another jar and plants two small blue circles in the centers of the whites. She outlines the ovals with a thin line of red, then outlines that in black, then finally sticks two pinprick-size black dots in the center. She stretches her forehead up again, leans closer (I hear her waist crack horribly), turns her head a little left, a little right. She looks so familiar suddenly. Like every older sister, every single sixth-grade tart-in-waiting, every racy cheerleader in the restroom, every single mom, like every female I have ever seen put on her makeup. And though Barbara doesn't blink, doesn't pucker up her lips to test the final look, she looks exactly like someone I used to know when I was young. But I can't place her.

She wipes the extra junk off her fingers, screws the lids back on the jars, closes the compact, and drops it all back in the purse. She looks at me with the self-conscious confidence of someone who's learned to cope with her terrible handicap. I realize I've been staring, open-jawed, and look away, ashamed.

I take a final swig of my beer and say, "Excuse me." I walk to the bar. I feel like a zombie. I can't make my legs move right. I feel so stiff. I get a cup of coffee and go to the phone. Three rings, then Pat's machine. "Pat. Can you please come down to the Rose? Please? I just saw something really bizarre. I feel a little weirded out. Please?"

I sit in the phone booth and take a few deep breaths. I count to ten. I count to ten again. I pull out my wallet and count my cash—seven bucks. No way I could have had more than two beers.

When I get back to the table I'm still feeling sluggy, but Barbara seems fine. She seems, in fact, terrific.

"You were asking about my friend," she says.

"Yeah, but you don't have to tell me—" I don't think I want to hear about her friend.

But Barbara's already talking.

Barbara doesn't know who her parents are. She can't remember any of her childhood. She only really remembers when she was already a teen. My stomach tightens thinking how the only way she could cope with what she went through as a child was to repress it. She does remember, though, as an early teen, being shunted from place to place, from home to home. Sometimes she had to go alone, but more often she was schlepped around in a crowd—a pack of three or four or more of them. They never had a choice where they were sent.

Then, under the guise of giving her a "comfortable home environment," the creeps she ended up with used her.

Her eyes (eye makeup?) glisten when she tells me horrifying stories of how they made her wear all these costumes. How they obsessively dressed and undressed and dressed her. She shakes when she tells me about the tennis suits, and nurses' dresses, the cheerleader skirts and jumpers, the pom-poms, the cheap black patent leather purses. The ball gowns and the swimsuits, and the nighties. The little teeny tiny bras and eensy little panties. How they ordered her to act like someone else, how they indulged their unrelenting fantasies: "Now you're a coed. Raise your hand." "Now you're a cheerleader. Jump." "Now you're a ballerina. Stretch." They never saw her as a person, just a thing. She was never safe around any of them. The adults would throw her in a box and stick her somewhere dark or throw her out. The girls would pull her hair out. The boys would tear off her clothes. They'd dunk her in the mud or hold her down in the disposal while they turned it on. Or paint her, head to toe, with nail polish. Or train their dogs to pick her up and throw her around and chew off her arms and legs. She remembers having her limbs yanked out, then crammed back in. And how many times they tried to mix and match her parts with someone else's: Joe's or Midge's or even—God forbid—Betsy's. Or something else entirely: Magic Markers, pens, Vienna sausages. She tells me about the scissors and the needles and the matches, glue and dirt. The places where they put her hands. The holes they put her head in.

She pauses while she sniffs and dabs her eyes. (Careful! I think, Careful!)

I know they say that talking about these things helps. It's listening to them I have problems with: I'm feeling a little queasy. I raise my hand to flag the waitron. I need a shot of something. Barbara hasn't even gotten to the cancer part of her story yet. I can't believe this poor woman's life has been one circle of hell below the last.

There was, however, one bright spot in her wretched life, one thing that kept her going: her "friend." Miraculously, despite the zillions of times she was hauled from one grubby kid's hands to some poking other's, she often was placed in the same home as her "friend." Barbara's voice quavers when she mentions the "friend." I hear her voice melt with love. She tells about how the two of them talked and listened to and comforted one another, how they understood, how they experienced and witnessed and remembered the cruel, unnatural things they were forced to do. She tells me that they vowed, like any pair of true loves from the halls of High Romance, that someday they would meet again, and live as they were meant to live, in freedom, independence, joy, and happiness. Forever.

I'm glad the bar is so crowded that no one else can hear her speech. It's just the kind of thing that would inspire some holdover hippie earth momma to twang out a spontaneous healing ballad.

It's taken Barbara's story this long to get around to her friend, to almost admitting why they chose the dyke bar for the scene of their reunion.

The thought of which reminds me of the long-late Pat. I excuse myself and go call her. I get the machine again. But this time the message is different:

"Hello, Brown. I know it's you. And so does the lovely coed I've been entertaining—fuckus interruptus— every single goddamn time you've called this evening. Didn't you get my message at the Rose that I was otherwise engaged? In answer to your questions: No, I will not bring her to the Rose. No, I don't need to meet your most recent social service project. And no no no I do not want you to call back later tonight, even if it is a matter of love and death, because I am bound and determined to lose my virginity again this very evening. But yes, dear, I still adore you, you asshole. And I'll call you soon. Tomorrow. Happy hunting." Click.

I put the phone back on the hook and laugh. Pat's always told me I'm the only person in the world she ever gets phone messages from. But I wish that tonight, this once-in-a-lifetime golden opportunity, her mom would call. Or her idiot ex-girlfriend. I laugh again, happy that she's finally managed to wrestle this cutie she's been morris-dancing around for months into the sack. I'm glad Pat's found, if only for tonight, a nice little Ginger. Fred. Whoever.

Then all of a sudden I get it about the voice. It wasn't the divine who called my name to lead me to talk to Barbara, it was one of the bar staff trying to tell me I had a phone message.

When I get back to the table I'm almost surprised to

see Barbara. I'd kind of hoped she'd have moved along. But she's still there—waiting to corner me behind the eight ball of her witty repartee.

"Want to see a picture of my friend?"

Not really, I think. But I smile anyway, thinking of Pat's finally getting some shaking in the sack. I guess Barbara reads that smile as a yes. She takes a photo from her purse and hands it to me.

I take the photo from between her fingers.

"The last place we were together was Colorado."

"Oh," I say.

"*Colorado,*" she insists, as if there's something significant I'm not getting.

So what's so special about Colorado? I wonder. The photograph is in the snow, the two of them standing in front of a ski lodge, bundled to the max. I can barely tell them apart at first. Then I see which one is Barbara. She's in some ludicrous ski bunny get-up. Her "friend" is taller, bigger-shouldered. Butch. But, like Barbara, is so covered in puffy ski clothes, I can't see much more than that. Suddenly I squint at them. How can they look, when there's so little I can see, so familiar? Barbara points to the picture and sniffs and dabs her eyes (Careful! Careful!).

"We both love skiing," she says. "That's about the only good that ever came of all those outfits . . . and skiing is one reason we decided to try our new life in Seattle. The mountains are so close. . . ."

Then she looks at me directly. She clears her throat. "You're probably wondering about my—" she chokes "—friend."

I've got you two figured out, I think. But I don't say anything. "What about your 'friend'?" I ask innocently.

"We—my friend and I—wanted—needed—to leave where we had lived and go someplace new. Where we could start anew. And since Seattle has a long history of liberal politics, fair employment for—minorities—and tolerance of—" she looks left the way a normal person would look down in her lap "—tolerance of 'alternate' marriages, we thought that we would try it here. You see, my friend is . . ."

She still can't manage to utter the syllable: gay. This is beginning to bug me.

A long awkward pause. I try to help her. "Why did your friend stay in Colorado when you came here?"

She looks the other way. "I wanted to settle in for us . . . and my friend had to stay in Colorado for . . ."

"For?"

She clears her throat. "Medical reasons."

Here comes the cancer, I think. Finally. But can it be that both of them are sick? Poor both of them! The pieces of my heart are breaking into crumbs.

She looks left and right again, then says, with measured calm, "My friend stayed for the operation."

What operation? I'm thinking. But it would be too forward, even for me, to ask directly.

She puts her hands in front of her on the table. I recognize the nervous pose of waiting.

I'm sitting facing the door. Barbara is facing me. So I'm the one who sees the door crash open and in stumble, on a pair of heels to write to the Department of Public Works about, this—person. And suddenly I understand Barbara's reluctance to use any gender-specific pronouns for her transitioning "friend." She's six eight if she's an inch. Shoulders that would make a sumo wrestler tremble. A Kirk Douglas chin, pork chop calves, and quarterback hands. She's wearing a tent of an acrylic flower-print dress, belt around the middle, and toting a black patent leather clutch—just like Barbara's!—beneath her elbow like a toolbox. Her hair is piled high as any menthol-puffing truck stop waitress. Her soft, yet rugged, face looks left and right, the same stiff way Barbara's does.

"I think your friend is here," I say.

Barbara swings her head left—then halfway around like in *The Exorcist*! She makes that "*-ck-ck*" sound again and I'm afraid she's going to choke again, but she doesn't. It turns into a little gasp of happiness, it sounds so sweet. I see her friend's eyes light with happiness.

And that look shoots through me with tenderness. That look is more endearing, more wholly tender, than anything I've ever seen in my whole life, in any Fred or Ginger, in any morning-after in my bed. I see in the look they give each other how hard-earned was the confidence, how great the leap of faith, that let them know, despite the cheap shots and the prejudice she faced throughout her life, that Barbara's friend had always been a woman trapped inside the body of a man, a dyke trapped in the body of a dreamboat. And I think how true, no, truer, is the patient love of this dear pair, who recognized each other's hearts, who willed their bodies stiffly wait until they got the bodies they were always meant to have.

And then I see before me how their bodies change.

When their eyes meet, Barbara stands, and her friend, who up till now has only turned her head left and right, *lifts* up her head, as if a spell were broken. Then Barbara takes a step—a real step—bending slightly at the knee, no longer stiff or sliding. Her rigid body is loosening. Her friend begins to stumble, but she doesn't fall, because her legs loosen too, and then she trots gracefully; she's suddenly as limber as a girl. The crowd divides between them like the water did for God. Then it's like we're in the last scene of a movie. Barbara and her friend spread their lovely arms out wide, and then, like in that old hair dye commercial, they're loping, slow-mo, knees and ankles bending, soft, luxurious, shiny, bright hair swinging. They fling their purses to the wind and stretch their arms and hands and fingertips to one another, and by the time they hold each other in their arms, their bodies are as smooth and supple, as pretty and romantic, as Fred and Ginger. Ginger and Ginger. Whoever. They swing each other around and look deep into one another's eyes—real eyes by now, real human, blinking, misty eyes—and sigh. The air around them turns to smoke, that purple stuff, like from the same hair dye commercial. Everything gets purple and thick, and I can't see anymore. But I can hear, like someone's stuck a mike down both their cleavages and hooked it up to me. I hear them call each other's names, I hear them name the lovers I remember:

"Barbie?"

"Ken?"

"Barbara."

"Ken-dra."

"Barbara!"

"Kendra!"

"Oh, Barbara!"

"Oh, Kendra!"

"Oh, Barbara!"

BARBIE

Jose Padua

I am Barbie.
I live in your dollhouse.
You change my clothes every day.

If I could get out
of here I would
kill you all.

HELL'S ANGEL BARBIE

Jeff Weddle

barbie's hog was
bad riding beside
sonny at the front
of the pack me tagging
behind sucking up fumes
but not minding cause
it gave me a great view
of barbie's cute behind
vibrating with the bike
i could tell she
was near climax
the way her harley
swerved almost into the
path of a semi and
back just in time
as she winked at me
in her rearview
and nudged sonny to pull
off near some bushes
i figured what the hell
there's more plastic
in the factory
almost glad
as the rest of us
whooped and gunned
our engines

racing forward to
kick ass on some
town in the cold
american night

CONFEDERATE BARBIE

Jeff Weddle

barbie was off somewhere
birthing a baby or some
such nonsense when sherman's
troops marched in and set
fire to everything
i'd just got back from belle's
place having my pipes cleaned
and whatnot
and i sat back for a julep
not giving a damn
about the blaze
as a yankee ran by with
barbie slung naked
across his shoulders
tits flapping in the soft
breeze semen running down
her thigh that glazed look
she sometimes gets underneath
her smile
and i couldn't
help myself i started
humming mine eyes
have seen the glory
mine eyes
mine eyes have
seen

BARBIE

Roberta Allen

On a television talk show, the host announced the guests for the following day. One of his guests, he said, would be a woman who spent fifty thousand dollars to look like a Barbie doll. But the woman, briefly on-screen, didn't look like Barbie to me. She didn't look plastic. After fifty thousand dollars worth of plastic surgery, the woman should at least look plastic even if she doesn't look like Barbie. But the woman looked like a flesh-and-blood woman. She had long hair, bangs, and a curvaceous figure. She wore a short skirt, high heels, and sunglasses. If no one had said she was supposed to look like Barbie, I bet no one would have seen a resemblance. But that's the reason for talk show hosts: how else would an audience with heads as empty as Barbie dolls know what they were seeing?

BEAUTY

L y n n e   B a r r e t t

Susan sat in her girlhood room in pajama bottoms and an old black bra, doing her pregnancy test. Not that she needed it. She was nine days late and already her breasts felt huge, swollen under her arms and strangely sensitive at the nipples. And she was so dizzy. Floors sponged underfoot. Pregnant at thirty-three from sex in a hatchback with a boy who couldn't be more than twenty-three, twenty-four.

It was 5:15 in the morning. Soon her mother would be up, filling the house with force.

She lay back on the carpet and looked up at the ranked figures of her thirty-three Barbies, each on her stand on the long white shelf, each costumed by Susan's mother in an outfit handmade to represent the year, beginning in 1959, her first birthday. From her earliest memory there they were, multiplying as she grew. When she'd complained—at twelve, thirteen—that she was too old for dolls, her mother went right on, planning, designing, sewing the annual costume exquisitely. She said, they're valuable. She said, someday they'll go to your little girl. And each time Susan left home, the dolls stayed here, waiting for her to screw up and return.

At eighteen she'd gone off to college and majored in theater arts. Her family told her this was foolish, squandering her expensive education, but she had been unable to pull away from the fascination of working on herself. She liked altering her letter *A*, waying the word *water* over and over. She turned out to have a gift for using makeup to delude people about the shapes of faces. In acting classes, she excelled at strong emotion—terror, rapture, and despair. When she landed a part, though (she played a deadly sin in *Everyman*), she found she had the necessary feeling but not the control to remember blocking at the same time. She was at her best just before the play, standing with the other actors in a circle, holding hands and opening up their throats, reciting *Bay Bee Buy Bow Beauty*.

Even with the reduced ambition of being a makeup artist, she had a rough time in New York. She walked dogs in all weathers, she stayed up late doing the makeup for a sixty-seven-year-old cabaret singer, she slept on the floor of the closet of an apartment on the Lower East Side, and finally she went home to Maryland with walking pneumonia and slept for two months.

A nice young man came after her and brought her back to share the wealth he was picking up on Wall Street. He thought having a wife in the theater was luxurious and didn't mind supporting her while she performed with a women's group that denounced patriarchy and sports. They rehearsed often, long improvisational sessions in which they complained about their crazy, awful, lovely, wasted mothers. They performed four times at a tiny theater that was really a SoHo living room, a piece called *Woman is Liquid* in which all she did was cry. Meanwhile the stock market crashed and she and her husband stopped being able to go out for dinner and then he told her he wanted her out of the way while he failed, even though she didn't at all mind failure, even though everyone she knew failed jauntily as a way of life. They divorced and she went back to Cumberland. From her marriage she retained some wonderful luggage and bad credit.

The dot on the stick was pink, positive. Susan buried the test in her closet, snapped the light off, and got back into bed. She waited for the bad feeling: pregnancy. Panic and sweat and some grim plan. Instead she laughed. It was hilarious, delicious. Probably that was hormones. She put her hands on her belly and felt nothing. But her breasts—they throbbed, they swelled, they pressed opulently against each other.

If I stay here, she thought, it will all be impossible. I'll fight with Mom, Dad will be kind but he'll feel disgraced, and my brothers will go after the boy—the poor boy. But I could take off. Go someplace new. Jemma is out in California; she said I should visit. Santa Cruz, wasn't it? I wonder if I can find that card. I can go out there and scrounge some kind of work and have the baby. Once there's a real baby, well, what can anyone say?

She pulled the covers up to her chin and went to sleep.

On their stands, the Barbies watched over her, with their sixty-six doe eyes.

"Lazy Susan, will you get up, will you get up, will you get up," her mother sang. The shades snapped, opening the morning. *Lazy Susan*: probably her earliest memory. And who knows how much damage that did? She stretched her legs under the quilt. Her mother was telling her to get a move on, it was 7:30 already, Dad had left for work, and she had to get out to the store after she gave Susan breakfast. She really doesn't think I can get my own breakfast, Susan thought. She doesn't think I can do anything. But what does she know? She hasn't the slightest suspicion. . . .

Susan drank orange juice, took a vitamin, and let her coffee go cold. For ten years she'd lived on coffee and now she couldn't stand it. She could swear she smelled chemicals in it, some taint of processing. She could detect preservatives in the strawberry jam. She sniffed through the refrigerator and chose orange marmalade—that was pure. While her mother was out of the room, watering the houseplants, she ate several spoonfuls of it and threw away her English muffin.

While her mother got groceries, Susan went through her clothes, picking out her biggest shirts and sweaters and tossing them on the bed. She went up to the attic to get the bags from Italy her husband had bought her, made of leather that only got more luscious with time. She shuffled through a stack of papers till she found Jemma's postcard with elephant seals on it, mating. The invitation was vague and there was no phone number, but they'd been roommates at school and she knew Jemma could stand her for a few days, anyway. After that, she'd find something. She laughed again. Her own optimism seemed funny to her. . . .

Then she was outside. (She kept losing chunks of time. It must be hormones.) She loaded her makeup collection, neatly packed in a set of vintage lizard travel cases, into the trunk of the Olds her father had passed along to her when she came home. He'd sweetly said it was a good excuse to buy a new car.

Her mother stormed up the driveway with a beep and jumped out to see what she was doing, crunching over the remnants of snow in the yard in her red rubber boots. It was another gray, gray, gray March day in Cumberland, wet and rusty. Susan became aware that she herself wore just a T-shirt, jeans, and leaky sneakers. But she wasn't cold at all. As she carried groceries inside, she carefully, cheerfully, presented the California plan. Lied and said Jemma had called at 10 (7 A.M. out there, you know) to beg her to come right away, there was a theater job. She'd have to leave first thing tomorrow morning. That would be wonderful, her mother said, a new start. And so tonight's dinner would be a farewell. She'd have all three of Susan's brothers over, if she could get them. There was a pot roast in the freezer.

Susan looked over towards the gap in the gray mountains that led west from Maryland. Her mother babbled. It was sad, really, that she knew Susan so little, that she didn't suspect a thing.

But if I told her, Susan thought, up in her room where she was sorting and folding clothes, I'd have to explain, over and over, the boy. And how to explain that? She'd volunteered for the job of doing makeup for a small college production of *Guys and Dolls*, just over the line in Virginia, teaching a couple of sessions on the craft of disguise, thinking she could at least put it on her resume. He'd been the one the others overlooked; that was the main thing. Hair too short and ill cut, skin poreless and transparent, changing color with each thought. No mask. The young girls didn't like that. She had shown them her greases and powders, secret mixtures and recipes for getting tints safely off the face again, and listened to their lament: no interesting guys. When she'd said, "Jeff?" they'd wrinkled their faces (messing up her work), dismissing him. Too straight, too serious. But Susan had seen his broad square back, his fine skin, and his capacity for devotion, not yet used up. The girls would rather have someone to complain of, though—and hadn't she once been like that herself?

After the show, taking his makeup off, she had covered his face in cream (he'd been one of the drunks at the mission, a character part, a complete transformation), and she'd gone in very close to take the wrinkles off his neck and—no one could see—she licked the hollow at his nape and watched the blush spread up his chest, his look of wonder in the mirror. "I like you," she'd said, matter-of-factly—it was that simple. Only then it turned out they were a pair, both living with parents, with no space of their own but cars, and in the hatchback of his she'd felt the condom split as he withdrew. It had been in his wallet, he said, a long time, at least a year and a half, two years. Disease, which was all they thought of in New York, seemed unlikely—he was so grateful and flustered. She'd forgotten to worry about this, the complication of health.

Her period had been due in two days. So the sperm had to survive time in the rubber and then clambered a long way, and the egg had lounged, holding up in her tube just enough. She knew dozens of women who had worked hard with calendar, thermometer, and drugs to do this. She felt the vanity of undeserved achievement.

At the bank, she nearly fainted. Once she had her money—eleven hundred dollars in traveler's checks—she wobbled outside and gasped. The air was steely. You wait, she told the thing inside her—a dragonfly, a pollywog, a smelt—I'll take you out of here to a place where the wind is a kind breath, where whales swim by.

Her mother was polishing the silver. The dining room table was unfurled for dinner with her brothers. Across it her mother had thrown an old sheet. She had out the Victorian coffeepot, sugar and creamer, silver-topped cruets, salt cellars, gravy boats, gill measures from the time of Paul Revere. Her mother's was a life spent in preparation and cleanup, with too little event.

Susan took a chair across from her. "I like doing this," her mother said, defensively. (Had she said anything? Had she questioned the worth of this chore?) "It lets me sit. Lately I'm so lazy."

"You're never lazy."

"Oh, yes, I'm so lazy—" She darted out to the kitchen to turn the heat down under the soup. "So lazy that sometimes—" She stood on her chair to pull a set of candlesticks from atop the hutch. (Susan felt ill looking up at her.) "So lazy that I look forward to going to the dentist because I can just sit still in that chair and *rest*."

"You're tired," Susan said, seeing, it seemed for the first time, the circles of blue-white skin under her mother's eyes. Veins popped across the backs of her hands as she polished the coffeepot.

"This was my grandmother's. Someday when you're married—I mean, married again, really married, you know, settled—it will be yours."

Susan thought, what if I said, right now, *I'm pregnant.* How astonished she would be.

"She was a great worker," her mother said. "She used to take all the rugs outside, this time of year, and beat them. Spring cleaning, you know. She used to say, your great-grandmother, that you could tell God was a male because he rested."

Susan had heard this many times, her mother's one joke, but now she got it. She saw the long line of women beating rugs and cooking banquets, who never fully shut their eyes at night; even in pain, in illness, they were alert, ready to jump up at a child's cry. They polished, scrubbed, ran their fingers into dusty corners, ironed, while they let men strut about work. Labor. A woman's word to start with.

In her room, Susan had to lie down among the piles of clothing on her bed. The Barbies stood tall on their ever-arching feet. She never played with them. Play was for lesser dolls named Tammy or Jenny, dolls who could be bashed, dirtied, denuded, who wound up bald and eyeless and beloved. Susan might touch Barbie's hair with a fingertip or fluff out a skirt, but even that could wear her, diminish her. The first one, 1959, wore the full skirt and prim blouse of a fifties housewife.

For a time they followed the spirit of each year, capturing 1962 in matched coat and hat and A-line dress, a lace-edged hankie in her tiny purse. 1964 wore mod dress and go-go boots, and 1967, Hippie Barbie, an India-print skirt with flecks of mirror. Her mother had put flowers in her hair, had made the tiny tie-dye T-shirt. She had strung red beads and researched the daishiki for 1968's Black Barbie, a mocha Barbie really. Her features were the same, of course, the nose no one could breathe through, the egret neck. Then her mother had moved from public history to private, reproducing Susan's riding habit from the year she'd been horse-mad, her prom dress, her off-to-college outfit of wool skirt and cowl-neck sweater, Barbie's knitted on size AA needles. The wedding gown—the real one was in the attic somewhere, but Barbie in hers looked fresh and hopeful. Virginal. But then, Barbie would stay intact through anything. Susan looked down at herself, so interestingly unintact. In August she would be thirty-four and five months pregnant. What would her mother make? There could be no maternity Barbie. Barbie could never change shape, thicken. Barbie, of course, was very, very careful.

After dinner, after her brothers—who lived nearby, owned together a business fixing up old houses, and still brought their laundry home—had left, her father carried her luggage down and fitted it into the car like pieces of a jigsaw puzzle. He had loved jigsaw puzzles, Susan recalled; when she was ten or so they'd spent long winter afternoons doing them, drinking hot chocolate with quiet pleasure. As they came in, she suggested they have some cocoa now. (At dinner she'd eaten nothing but the mashed potatoes.) Her mother fussed at them for dirtying a pot she'd just scrubbed and sent them into the living room. Susan settled on the carpet in front of the fire, enjoying the old sensation of heat on one cheek and the untraceable draft of cold air on the other. Her father talked about his time in San Diego during World War II and how he'd been sure California was full of promise. I'll have him visit, she told herself, after the baby . . . She drained the sweet silt at the bottom of her cup and her father said, "You're looking very pretty," and hummed a bit, *A pretty girl is like a melody*, the song he used to sing when she came downstairs dressed to go to a dance or party. Her mother would immediately find some detail amiss—a thread loose, slip showing, the hopeless un-symmetrical wave of her hair. One afternoon, just before she married, her husband-to-be had said, "Doesn't she look great?" and her mother answered, "That skirt does disguise your bottom." And Susan had taken that as praise.

Her mother came in to take the cups away. Susan noticed—now she would always notice—those blue-white weary circles, the way her lipstick had worn into tiny crevices.

And her secret gave her power.

"I want to take the dolls," she told her mother.

"The dolls?"

"The Barbies. I would like to take them with me. You'll never ship them for fear they'd get lost. So let me take them. They are mine?"

"Of course." Her mother had to say, "Of course." And she went into a fury of packing. She decided it wouldn't do to have them travel dressed—the clothes would rumple—so she stripped each one and laid the clothes out on Susan's bed-spread. Each doll she tagged with her year and a clue to her outfit, rolled in tissue, and put into a large shopping bag. The Barbies weren't as interesting, Susan saw, as the outfits. Arrayed on the bed, they were something new, a work of art or anthropology. Their lines so sharp, their details so exacting, as if her mother had been sewing herself into the moment. They represented her mother's strenuous vision of perfection.

"They're beautiful," she told her mother.

"You'll probably get them all mixed up," she snapped.

Her mother put each set of clothes into a Baggie. "Be sure to get them out of these as soon as you can," she said. "Plastic isn't good for fabric. And *wash* them. When textiles get dirt in them, they rot." Susan nodded all through a lecture on soaking and detergents and how to use an iron, aware that she was taking something important away from her mother. But she'll forgive me, she thought, when she knows about the baby.

They put the clothes into another shopping bag and Susan promised to watch them every second, to take them inside with her when she stayed in motels, to avoid strong light, or heat, or cold. She minds their going, Susan thought, so much more than mine.

On the other side of the Cumberland Gap—West!—light flurries whirled around the car. Susan drove into West Virginia. At noon she stopped at a scenic overlook where nothing could be seen but snow. She had packed a cooler with bottled water and liverwurst sandwiches. She never liked liverwurst before, but now she craved its smoothness, its blend of fat and iron. Liverwurst on rye. She started the car, still chewing, and drove into more snow. On into Kentucky, it turned to rain. The car got stuffy. She rolled down the window and warm wet air blew in. She smelled mud. She flew to the rhythm of the car, the wipers, the occasional lurch of her stomach. The radio played static, signs whistled by. Who knew what time it was? She reached into the bag beside her, pulled a doll from its nest of tissue, held it in her hand. Thin, hard, light. She balanced it like a weapon and then flicked it out the window. She laughed. It must be hormones. Through late afternoon, early twilight, every hundred miles or so, she flung another Barbie into the rush of air. The night turned foggy, but she would make it all the way to the Mississippi before she paused. Inside her the baby whirred, translucence with a heartbeat.

And behind her the Barbies took root and grew tall, casting their beautiful shadows over the land.

BARBIE'S SHOES

Hilary Tham

I'm down in the basement
sorting Barbie's shoes:
    sequin pumps, satin courts,
    western boots, Reebok sneakers,
    glass slippers, ice-skates, thongs.
All will fit the dainty, forever arched
feet of any one Barbie: Sweet Spring
    Glitter-eyed, Peaches and Cream,
    a Brazilian, Russian, Swiss, Hong Kong
    Hispanic or a Mexican, Nigerian
    or Black Barbie. All are cast
in the same mold, same rubbery,
impossible embodiment of male fantasy
with carefully measured
    doses of melanin to make
      a Caucasian Barbie,
        Polynesian Barbie
        African-American Barbie.
Everyone knows that she is the same
Barbie and worthy of the American Dream
House, the Corvette, opera gloves, a
hundred pairs of shoes to step into. If only
the differently colored men and women we know
could be like Barbie, always smiling, eyes
wide with admiration, even when we yank
off an arm with a hard-to-take-off dress.
Barbie's shoes, so easily lost, mismatched,
useless; they end up, like our prejudices,
in the basement, forgotten as spiders
sticking webs in our darkest corners,
we are amazed we have them still.

ABOUT THE AUTHORS

ROBERTA ALLEN is the author of *The Traveling Woman* stories; *The Daughter*, a novella-in-stories; *Amazon Dream*, an alternative travel book. She is also a conceptual artist who has exhibited worldwide, with artwork in the collection of the Metropolitan Museum of Art. She lives in New York City.

JULIA ALVAREZ left the Dominican Republic when she was ten years old. In 1986 she published her first book of poetry, *Homecoming*. She is the author of the highly acclaimed novel, *How the García Girls Lost Their Accents*.

LYNNE BARRETT has published a collection of short stories, *The Land of Go*. In 1991 she won the Edgar Award for the best mystery short story. She lives and writes in Miami, Florida.

JEANNE BEAUMONT is a free-lance medical editor in New York City. Her poetry has appeared in *Poetry*, *The Nation*, *Gettysburg Review*, and *Boulevard*.

REBECCA BROWN lives in Seattle, Washington. She is the author of two novels, *The Haunted House* and *The Children's Crusade*. Her most recent book is a linked collection of stories, *The Terrible Girls*. Her work has been well received in England and translated into Dutch and German. She is looking for a publisher for another short story collection, *Grief & Other Short Stories*.

SANDRA CISNEROS is the author of *Woman Hollering Creek*, a collection of short stories; *The House on Mango Street*, a novel; and two collections of poetry, *My Wicked Wicked Ways* and *Bad Boys*. She lives in San Antonio, Texas.

LAURA COSTAS is primarily a graphic artist. She has written for *Regardie's* and has one unpublished novel and a second on the way.

DENISE DUHAMEL has published three poetry chapbooks: *Heaven and Heck, It's My Body*, and *Skirted Issues*. A recipient of a New York Foundation of the Arts Fellowship, she has had residencies at the MacDowell Colony, Yaddo, and the Helene Wurlitzer Foundation.

RICHARD GRAYSON, a Brooklyn native, is the author of five books of fiction, including *With Hitler in New York* and *I Brake for Delmore Schwartz*. He has taught writing and computer education courses at a dozen colleges in New York and South Florida.

CATHRYN HANKLA is the author of a collection of stories, *Learning the Mother Tongue*; a novel, *A Blue Moon in Poorwater*; and two volumes of poetry, *Phenomena* and *Afterimages*. She teaches in the writing program at Hollins College in Virginia.

KATHRYN HARRISON attended Stanford University and the University of Iowa Writer's Workshop. In 1989 she was awarded a James Michener fellowship. *Thicker Than Water* is her first novel.

SHARON HENRY is completing her first novel.

LISA B. HERSKOVITS has a useless M.F.A., was born and raised in Cleveland, Ohio, and resides semihappily in New York City. She publishes *Bikini Girl* magazine.

A. M. HOMES holds an M.F.A. from the University of Iowa Writer's Workshop and has received, among other awards, a James Michener Fellowship, a New York Foundation for the Arts Fellowship, and a Henfield Transatlantic Review Award. She is the author of a novel, *Jack*, and a collection of stories, *The Safety of Objects*.

WAYNE E. KLINE lives in Manassas, Virginia. His book of poems is entitled *Asbestos*.

PHILIP LEVINE is a distinguished poet who has won the Lenore Marshall Award, the National Book Critics Circle Award, the American Book Award, and the National Book Award for his poetry books. His most recent book is *Nice Work*.

LYN LIFSHIN is the author of over seventy books. Recent titles include: *Kiss the Skin Off*, *Rubbed Silk*, and *The Doctor Poems*. She has edited a series of books on women's writing: *Tangled Vines*, *Ariadne's Web*, and *Unsealed Lips*. She is also the subject of the recent documentary *Not Made of Glass*.

COOKIE LUPTON lives in Arlington, Virginia. Her poems have appeared in the *Provincetown Paper* and the *Boston Reader*.

ALICE McDERMOTT currently teaches at American University. She is the author of *A Bigamist's Daughter*, *That Night*, and *At Weddings and Wakes*.

LYNNE McMAHON teaches at the University of Missouri in Columbia, Missouri. She has received an Ingram Merrill Award and a Missouri Arts Council grant. Her book of poems, *Faith*, was published in 1988. She recently completed a new manuscript tentatively titled *Develoution of the Nude*.

JOSE PADUA lives in New York City and is the coeditor of *Big Cigars*.

MARGE PIERCY has written nine novels, including *Gone to Soldiers* and *Small Changes*, and has published eleven collections of poetry. Her work has been translated into fourteen languages.

ELLIE SCHOENFELD lives on a hill in Duluth, Minnesota, overlooking Lake Superior. She is cofounder of Poetry Harbor, an organization that produces monthly readings and weekly poetry programs for television. Her poetry has appeared in *Poetry Motel*, *Asylum*, *Bogg*, *Hippo*, and in two anthologies: *Poets Who Haven't Moved To Minneapolis* and *Poets Who Haven't Moved To St. Paul*.

GREGG SHAPIRO has had fiction in *Christopher Street*, *Thing*, and the *Washington Blade*, and poetry in *Gargoyle*, *The Quarterly*, *Asylum*, *Mudfish*, *Widener Review*, *Lip Service*, and *Plum Review*. His work, along with that of two other poets, is featured in *Troika II* (Thorntree Press). Now living in Chicago, he is a cofounding member of SoPo Writers and coeditor of *Queer Planet Review*.

LESLIE SHIEL has been published in *New Virginia Review* and *Richmond Quarterly*. She holds an M.F.A. from Virginia Commonwealth University, where she now teaches.

GARY SOTO teaches in the English Department at U.C. Berkeley, and is the author of seven volumes of poetry, the most recent being *Home Course Religion*.

SPARROW lives in New York City and hasn't eaten pastrami for twenty-one years.

PATRICIA STORACE, a native of Mobile, Alabama, was educated at the Madeira School, Barnard College, and the University of Cambridge. Her poetry has appeared in *Parnassus*, *Agni Review*, *Har-*

per's, and *The Paris Review*, to name a few. *Heredity* is her first collection of poetry.

BELINDA SUBRAMAN lives in El Paso, Texas, where she has just finished editing *The Gulf War: Mini Perspectives*, which represents attitudes and experiences that were not covered by, or popular with, the media. Her poetry has appeared in *Yellow Silk* and the anthologies *Lips Unsealed* (Capra Press) and *A Geography of Poets* (University of Oklahoma).

HILARY THAM was born in Kelang, Malaysia. She lives in Arlington, Virginia, with her husband and three daughters and teaches creative writing in high schools. Her poetry volumes are *No Gods Today*, *Paper Boats*, *Bad Names for Women*, and *Tigerbone Wine*.

DAVID TRINIDAD is the author of six books of poetry, including *Hand Over Heart*, *November*, and *Monday, Monday*. His poetry has appeared in *City Lights Review*, *New American Writing*, and *BOMB*. Originally from Los Angeles, Trinidad now lives in New York City.

JOHN VARLEY burst onto the science fiction scene in the late 1970s. He's won both the Hugo and Nebula awards for his writing. His books include *Titan*, *Wizard*, *Millennium*, *Demon*, *The Persistence of Vision*, and *Blue Champagne*.

JEFF WEDDLE is a Ph.D. student in English at the University of Mississippi. He coedits the poetry magazine *Misnomer*, and has been everything from a movie projectionist to a short-order cook.